Radical Focus

ACHIEVING YOUR MOST IMPORTANT GOALS WITH OBJECTIVES AND KEY RESULTS

Christina Wodtke

 First Publishing Date, Beta Version under title "The Executioner's Tale," March 2014. First Edition of Radical Focus published January 2016.

ISBN-13: 978-0-9960060-2-6

DEDICATION

Dedicated to the dreamers, always unsatisfied, always sure the next time it will actually be good.

Dedicated to the executioners, who know the way to make things happen is to make them happen.

Dedicated to my beta readers, who made me think maybe this could be a book.

Dedicated to the editors of the world. Without you, I'd look dumb.

And, as always, dedicated to Amelie. Because Amelie.

CONTENTS

FOREWARD

When Performance Is Measured By Results

By Marty Cagan, Founder of the Silicon Valley Product Group

I was extremely fortunate to have started my career at Hewlett-Packard as an engineer during their heyday, when they were known as the industry's most successful and enduring example of consistent innovation and execution. As part of HP's internal engineering management training program called "The HP Way," I was introduced to a performance management system known as "MBO" - Management by Objectives.

The concept was straightforward and based on two fundamental principles. The first can easily be summed up with the famous General George Patton quote: "Don't tell people how to do things, tell them what you need done and let them surprise you with their results." The second was captured by HP's tagline of that era, "When Performance Is Measured By Results." The idea here is that you can release all the features you want, but if it doesn't solve the underlying business problem, you haven't really solved anything.

The first principle is really about how to motivate people to get them to do their best work, and the second in all about how to meaningfully measure progress.

So much has changed since my time at HP. The technologies are dramatically more advanced, the scale and scope of systems we build is several orders of magnitude larger, teams move much faster, generally with superior quality and performance, all delivered at a fraction of the cost. However, these two performance management principles are still at the foundation of how the best companies and teams operate.

The MBO system was refined and improved at several companies over the years, most notably Intel, and today the primary performance management system we use is known as the "OKR" system - Objectives and Key Results.

Unfortunately, another thing that hasn't changed is that most teams still don't operate with these principles.

Instead, groups of executives and other stakeholders all too often come up with the quarterly "roadmap" of features and projects and then pass them down to the product teams, essentially telling them how to solve the underlying business problems. The teams are just there to flesh out the details, code and test, with little understanding of the bigger context, and even less belief that these are in fact the right solutions. Teams today are all too often feature factories, with little regard for whether or not the features actually solve the underlying business problems. Progress is measured by output and not outcome.

This book is intended to help all organizations start operating like the best organizations. I have seen these techniques deployed successfully in organizations as large as a 60,000 employee company to as small as a 3 person startup. Large or small, if you've worked hard to hire smart people, this system will help you unleash their potential.

- Marty Cagan, Founder of The Silicon Valley Product Group (www.svpg.com)

INTRODUCTION

Every published writer has had it - the people who come up to you and tell you that they've Got An Idea. And boy, is it a Doozy. It's such a Doozy that they want to Cut You In On It. The proposal is always the same - they'll tell you the Idea (the hard bit), you write it down and turn it into a novel (the easy bit), the two of you can split the money fifty-fifty.

— Neil Gaiman, *Where Do you Get Your Ideas?*

In my years in the Silicon Valley, I've had a similar experience to Neil Gaiman's: I sit down with a new entrepreneur with "a big idea" and they ask me to sign an NDA. A nondisclosure agreement usually swears the parties to not talk about the ideas or copy them These kids are convinced that their idea is so precious and amazing that the hard work has been done. Nothing left to get a'coding!

I usually refuse. Ideas, like NDAs, aren't worth the paper they are printed on.

I almost never hear a new idea. In fact, it's rare I hear an idea I haven't thought of myself, unless it's in an industry I'm unfamiliar with. It's not because I'm a genius (I'm not). It's that ideas are easier to come up with than you think. What's hard—really hard—is moving from an idea to reality. It's hard to find the right form of an idea, a form that will let consumers see its value, understand how to interact with it, and feel excited enough to pay for it. That is so hard that it often takes a team of people to do it. And that's when the level of hard goes even higher. Suddenly you have to find a way to hire the right people, get them all focused on the right thing and make sure no one forgets why they got together in the first place in this world of interesting (and profitable) other things to do.

The writers. The musicians. They struggle, and they only have to manage themselves! The filmmakers and the entrepreneurs have even a greater challenge. Yet somehow these people manage to fight against the long odds against them to make their idea take form. How do they do it, when so many other fail to make it past the "I've got an idea!" stage?

It's not important to protect an idea. It's important to protect the time it takes to make it real.

You need a system to keep you—and your team—aimed at your goal when the world seems determined to throw shiny objects at you.

The system I use is made up of three simple parts. One: set inspiring and measurable goals. Two: make sure you and your team are always making progress toward that desired end state. No matter how many other things are on your plate. And three: set a cadence that makes sure the group both remembers what they are trying to accomplish and holds each other accountable.

Inspiring and Measurable Goals

I use OKRs for goal setting. I'll go into those in detail throughout the book. In short, this is a system originated at Intel and used by folks such as Google, Zynga, LinkedIn, and General Assembly to promote rapid and sustained growth. O stands for Objective, KR for Key Results. Objective is what you want to do (Launch a killer game!), Key Results are how you know if you've achieved them ("Downloads of 25K/Day," "Revenue 50K/Day"). OKRs are set annually and/or quarterly and unite the company behind a vision.

The Objective is inspiring and motivates those people who don't dig numbers. For those who do love numbers, the Key Results keep the Objective real. I know I've got a good Objective when you leap out of bed in the morning eager to make it happen. I know I've got the right Key Results when you are also a little scared you can't make them.

Tying Actions to Goals

When I first started learning about productivity systems, I heard of the Important/Urgent matrix. It's a simple four-square with two axes. The first is important and unimportant. The second is urgent and not urgent. We should spend time in important-and-urgent and do. We should spend time in important-but-not-urgent and *not* in unimportant-but-urgent, yet… urgent is so…

urgent! It's mentally quite difficult to drop things that don't matter (especially if someone is nagging us). So a solution is to time-constrain things that are important but not urgent, thus making them urgent.

Let's start with a personal example. Let's say you have been meaning to sign up for a personal trainer because you suck at getting to the gym. Yet week after week goes by and it never seems to happen. You could try making your health an Objective for a quarter, and Key Results involve muscle mass, weight and emotional well-being. Each Monday you set three tasks to complete against the goal. One might be "Call a personal trainer." Next you find someone to hold you responsible. A friend, a coach or a spouse are all good picks. Now, if you don't complete it, you will be held responsible by someone.

In a work example, it might be any number of things, from optimizing a database to creating a faster site and increasing customer satisfaction, to redoing all your material with the new brand so your company doesn't look unprofessional. The OKRs set goals. The weekly priorities remind you to achieve them.

As well, if you review the priorities each week, you discover what conditions allow you to achieve them. And, more valuable, what keeps you from getting things done. In my experience, many people fall into two camps of misestimating: those who think they can do anything and constantly overestimate what they'll accomplish and those who sandbag. As a manager, learning who is who lets me know who to push and who to question. As well, tracking lets the employee learn to know themselves better, a good outcome all by itself.

Cadence

Starting every week with a public setting of priorities is powerful. You commit to the team and to each other to make the Objective occur. A Friday celebration of what's been accomplished is the second bookend of a high-performing team's week. This commit/celebrate cadence creates a habit of execution.

Beware Greeks Throwing Golden Apples

When I was a kid, one of my favorite Greek myths was that of Atalanta. She was the fastest runner in Sparta and did not care to be married. Her father, being worse than medieval—ancient Greek—did not agree to that plan and set up a contest in which young men would race to win her hand in marriage. She begged to also race, to keep her freedom. Her father agreed, to keep her placid, never thinking she might win.

The day of the race, she was so amazingly swift, she might have won. Except a clever lad, Hippomenes, managed to lay hands on three golden apples and rolled them into her path each time she started to pull ahead. She kept pausing to pick them up, and Hippomenes beat her by a nose. If she had only set some clear goals and stuck to them, she might be ruling the city footloose and fancy free!

Every startup will run into golden apples. Maybe it's a chance to take stage at an important conference. Maybe it's one big customer that asks you to change your software for them. Maybe it's the poisoned apple of a bad employee who distracts you while you wring your hands over what to do about him. A startup's enemy is time, and the enemy of timely execution is distraction.

By setting good goals and committing to working toward them each week, while celebrating your victories, a company can have amazing and focused growth. No matter what kind of apples roll across their path.

The Executioner's Tale

My book is a fable of a small startup that almost didn't make it. Hanna and Jack start out as dreamers. They start out being really good at having an idea. They are good at hoping everything will work out well. They soon find out that a good idea is not enough: they need a system for making dreams happen.

By the end of the tale, they are no longer just dreamers. They are executioners.

THE EXECUTIONER'S TALE

Hanna sat at her desk, hunched over her keyboard, her shiny black bob hiding her face from the rest of the office. To them, perhaps, their young CEO looked like she was focused on the monitor. Perhaps going over last quarter's numbers, which were not anything like what they should be. But she wasn't looking at any number in the Excel sheet she had open. Her hands sat flat on either side of her keyboard, and only she knew she was trying hard not to face-plant into it. How the hell did she get here?

The company had a viable market but couldn't figure out how to get out of its own goddamn way and grab it. Her partner was a whiny diva. Her new CTO was some kind of methodology cultist, and she was going to have to fire someone for the first time in her too-short career.

Why had she wanted to be an entrepreneur, again?

SIX MONTHS AGO....

Once upon a time there was a startup.

This startup had a vision to bring delicious artisanal loose-leaf tea to fine restaurants and discerning cafés.

There were two founders, Hanna and Jack. Hanna was first-generation Chinese American and loved the tea she grew up with at her parents' house. Her mother had run a small restaurant in downtown Phoenix for years, and her family cared about good food and good tea. She studied business at the Stanford Graduate School of Business, and she hadn't been so lucky finding nice tea in Palo Alto. Hanna despaired of getting a nice cup of Longjing after a fine meal.

Jack was British and he was miserable at cafés that could poach an egg perfectly yet thought Earl Grey was a who and not a what. Jack was at Stanford, too, studying the design of Human-Computer Interaction. Jack loved technology when it meant carrying fewer books in his book bag or a spell check that caught his sloppy typing. But he drew the line at tea in little bags. He did not consider that progress.

Hanna and Jack met one day at the university bookstore café. Jack was loudly moaning over tea in packets. Hanna, standing behind him in line, laughed and showed him the tin of green tea she had in her purse. They quickly became friends. Hanna had known she would be an entrepreneur since she was a little girl. She came from a family of entrepreneurs. Besides her mother's restaurant, her father had his own accountant's office, and Hanna's aunt had started her own law firm.

Entrepreneurship was in her genes. She hadn't known what kind of company she wanted to start until she met Jack. They agreed to take an entrepreneurship course the spring of their senior year, and after graduation they were ready to go.

Jack and Hanna knew there were plenty of great tea producers. So they decided they would connect the people who grew great tea with fine restaurants and cafés that were snobbish about coffee but ambivalent about tea. They named their startup TeaBee. And because they went to Stanford and had made the right connections, they managed to raise a little money to make a go at it.

Hanna took on the title of CEO and Jack that of President, but really Hanna owned the business and Jack the product. They found a small office near Highway 101 where the rents weren't quite as bad, and had a happy six months furnishing the office and giving away tea at tech meet-ups. They hired a few engineers, and Jack made a very pretty website where buyers could find tea producers and order tasty tea. Hanna closed a few deals with local restaurants. Jack talked Hanna into hiring a visual designer on contract to make a sexy logo, and they even got a part-time CFO to make sure the books balanced. The office hummed quietly with keyboards typing and murmurs of voices.

But they started to feel a little uneasy. While they had another year of money before they'd need to raise another round of funding, they still worried about why it was taking so long to build a marketplace. They had many, many little tea producers signing up, but only a few buyers. A lopsided market is not a profitable market. Like good founders, they decided to go out to try to sell more tea themselves, in order to learn more about the psychology of buyers.

One day, Hanna came back to the office with a very big order from a restaurant supplier. This restaurant supplier sold tea to all kinds of restaurants, big *and* small, as well as canned goods, dry goods and coffee. Jack was both happy and alarmed. He was happy to see so much money about to come into the business, yet this was not "to plan." They were here to connect fine dining and fine tea! Did this restaurant supplier care about tea? Did it care about quality?

"Jack," Hanna sighed. "The restaurants don't want to set up accounts with us. We're too new. They don't trust us. The suppliers are more willing to try us out, and they will place our tea in restaurants. The tea growers still get more business. Let's just see how this plays out."

HANNA FINDS ANOTHER GREAT CUSTOMER

A few days later, Hanna used her mother's Rolodex to close another deal with another restaurant supplier. She pulled into the parking lot outside their office and sat in the warm car for a moment, her hand on the keys still in the ignition. TeaBee's mission was "Bringing great tea to people who love it." Perhaps not the sexiest mission, but clear, she thought. Did it matter if she sold to a restaurant or a restaurant supply company? It shouldn't, she decided. She pocketed her keys and headed into the office.

The office was warmed by the same sun that made her car a bad place to hide. Hanna threw her blazer over the back of her Herman Miller chair. They'd bought the iconic chairs, as well as a couple of white boards, at a sale held by a startup that had run out of money. All startups are built with the bones of the past failures. Google's offices were once Netscape's were once Silicon Graphics'. You had to be optimistic or crazy to ignore the proof that launching a startup had only slightly better odds than winning the lotto. Hanna figured she and Jack were a bit of both.

She found Jack in the back of the office, where they had a long table set up. The team had lunch together there and held impromptu meetings when their one conference room was occupied. Jack stood next to the new designer he had just hired. Ann? No, Anya. Jack slouched to try to have an easier conversation with her. He was about six-two, and towered over little Anya's five-five. Hanna joined them, and Jack straightened a bit with a sigh.

On the table before them sat several cardboard boxes with different colored labels on them. "Hanna, have a look. I think this blue is rather lovely, but I'm afraid it won't pop on the shelf. This orange is stronger, but maybe it's not a tasty color? Blue is terribly trustworthy." Jack could talk about colors for hours. Add in typefaces, and you could lose half a day. Hanna had no idea why he thought they had needed to hire a graphic designer. Jack seemed knowledgeable enough. But he'd insisted it wasn't his bag, and she'd given in. Anya pushed forward a dark red box.

"Um, yes, the dark red is nice," Hanna said. "I'm sure you two have it under control. Jack, I just wanted to let you know… I closed Brightwater Supplies. They cover Modesto through Fresno."

Jack scrunched up his brow. "Fresno is... north?"

Hanna laughed out loud. "South! You are so coming with me next time I head into the Valley." She pushed aside the packaging mockups and placed the contract on the table in front of Jack. She flattened it out, almost as petting it. Jack looked it over. The numbers were… impressive. Bigger than any deal they had closed so far.

"Hey, this." He tapped at a spot in the contract where lines had been crossed out, and new bit written in. "What's this about not using the website?"

"It's too much work for them."

"Rubbish! I did usability testing on that."

"They looked at it and didn't like it. Don't freak out. You can go with me to see them in a couple weeks, when we do the check in. I'll just enter the orders in myself until you can figure out what the changes need to be. Perhaps you can get Erik to write an API so they can integrate it with their system? They order a lot of tea, and they order regularly."

Jack looked unconvinced.

"It's a boat-load of money and I'll do the work." Hanna took a deep breath. "Go back to work; don't fret."

She strode off to the kitchen to make a cup of tea, feeling upset. She had expected Jack to be excited. This was money. Not just money, but regular, hefty amounts of money. Yet he acted like she had brought in groceries but forgotten the milk. She felt better, though, as soon as she entered the kitchen. The room was full of the tea samples from the growers, and she was always spoiled for choice. She poked through a pile of samples of green tea from a Washington farm she's visited last week. She closed her eyes and pressed her nose into the bag, inhaling the scent of the tea, sweet, like dried grasses crushed underfoot on a hike. Then realized she wasn't alone.

"Ok, that's embarrassing," she said, turning to Jack.

He waved his hands. "Oh, whatever. We all do that. Tenzo's stuff is aces." He plugged in the electric kettle, and pulled another mug off the shelf. He leaned against the counter and crossed his arms across his chest. "I'm not sure I'm good with these people."

"These people?"

"Suppliers. They put Lipton into three-star restaurants. They don't *care*."

"I don't know about that. They provide what the restaurants want. I convince them good restaurants want good tea. It's just customer development." She shrugged.

"The point of a startup is to do things the right way. Excellent product, packaged excellently, sold to excellent customers. Not doing things the way everyone has been doing it."

"I thought the point of a startup was to find product/market fit in order to grow a company that benefits the people who depend on it."

The kettle light went on, and Jack poured. "Yeah, yeah, that's what it says in the textbooks. It doesn't matter if you can sell, if you sell rubbish." He swirled the tea ball around for emphasis. "This is our chance to make a *difference*. We can make amazing experiences even more amazing. I know you are worried about the bottom line. Just don't forget what we are all about." He strode from the room, not waiting for her answer.

We're *about* ten months from running out of money, unless we close more deals, Hanna thought. If the tea is good, and the money is good, what is the problem?

HANNA SUGGESTS A PIVOT

A few weeks later, Hanna pulled Jack into their conference room. The room was nothing special. It had the proportions of a shoebox and was painted the shade of white landlords seem to favor. Three of the four walls held elderly whiteboards, marred with traces of notes left by former tenants. Hanna found the florescent lighting mildly unpleasant, but at least didn't flicker. Hanna had been in many rooms just like this in the two years she'd spent consulting between college and grad school. Those with flickering lights had made her crazy. It was not only annoying on its own, but a sign the owners were too neglectful or distracted to deal with them. She considered them an omen of doom.

Upon entering their well-lit conference room, they found it occupied by Erik, their lead programmer. He liked to sit in the windowless room and code.

"Um, Erik, we need the room."

"One second…" Erik did not raise his sandy blond head from the laptop. Taller than Jack but much thinner, his lean frame formed a question mark over the gleaming silver computer.

"Sod off, Erik," Jack said, not unkindly, but firmly.

"Yes, going... I'm standing up... I'm walking." Erik rose, balancing the laptop on one arm, occasionally hitting a key. He exited without taking his eyes off the screen.

"Why does he hide in here?" Hanna felt irritable. She hoped Jack knew already what she was about to talk to him about, but she also had a bad feeling he didn't. Nor would he like it when he did.

Jack shrugged. "He needs to focus. Anyhow, he's good, and we don't have a CTO yet..."

This reminded Hanna of yet another problem. Technically, finding a CTO was on Jack's to-do list. But it seemed to Hanna that Jack didn't take interest in any part of the business that wasn't about design, and she wondered if she'd have to add it to her to-do list. She bit her lower lip.

They pulled up chairs at one end of the long conference table made up of two Ikea wooden kitchen counters Jack, Erik and their front-end developer Cameron had assembled one weekend, which made a handsome and affordable table. Unfortunately, they hadn't finished it, and anything spilled left a history. Hanna rubbed at a coffee stain with her finger while she figured out how to explain what she was thinking. The stain didn't fade.

Jack waited. Jack was good at silence.

"Jack, I've made several sales recently to restaurant suppliers." Hanna paused and Jack folded his arms across his chest. Ok, this wasn't going to go super easy. "Each sale has been the equivalent of closing ten to 20 restaurants. Because that's who they serve. I've been putting in the numbers for Aramaxx, and they are providing a lot of business for the tea producers. Jefferson Supplies has doubled their order. It's been so good, Tenzo Farms is even talking about adding staff!"

It seemed like Jack grew stiffer as she looked at him. She really hoped he'd just guess where she was going. Unless he had, and he didn't like it. Forward, then.

"This is a far better business. The sales cycles are just as long, but the suppliers are willing to try us out. Unlike the restaurants and cafés, where we can have five or ten meetings and they just want us to come back when we've been in business longer. I think we've got the evidence we need. I think it's time to pivot."

In their entrepreneurship class, they had learned that a pivot is a change in tactics without making a change in strategy. Hanna felt strongly this was exactly what needed to happen. They could still get great tea into the hands of consumers; they just needed to use the pre-existing relationships the restaurant suppliers had to do it.

Jack rocked back on his heels, nervously. "Look, I get it, about the sales cycle." He looked pleased with himself as he used the business jargon. "But I'm not at all sure the restaurant suppliers won't get the producers used to the custom, then try to push the prices down. What if they force the tea people to lower quality? What if they make garbage?"

Hanna chided him. "Solve the problems you have, not the ones you imagine." She had heard that a hundred times from her mother and laughed at herself for saying it now. "Jack, it's working. We are making the tea growers money. We are starting to make us money. And the suppliers will get dependent on us also. If it's mutually beneficial, they can't force us to do what we don't believe in."

Jack paused and closed his eyes for a second. She saw his eyes move under his lids, as if he was dreaming. He did that sometimes, when he worked on a design. It was him working a problem through to the end. He opened his eyes.

"Whose labels will go on the boxes?"

"Really?" Her eyes widened. "That's a worry?"

"We've done a lot of work on it. We need a brand presence. Like Intel on laptops. It made them. You can't settle for being a secret sauce!"

"I don't know what they are thinking on packaging. They haven't asked for us to change." She shrugged.

"Hmm. Well. I can see your point." His tone had Hanna far from convinced he did see her point. She noted he was grinding his teeth. "I think it might make sense to consider focusing on the suppliers." And there was his reluctant dance around the idea. Next would come the 'but.' "But look, you don't know, and I don't know, what it's going to be like, working with these blokes."

And, out of facts, Hanna was stuck. She couldn't argue with nebulous fears and vague anxieties. Then she had an idea.

"Let's talk to Jim."

Jim Frost had been the first angel who had invested in them. He was a Valley veteran, and had seen many companies go under, as well as a few succeed. He was wise and insightful and, if anyone could help them figure this out, it'd be Jim. Jack and Hanna had both learned to trust him. He had introduced them to their lead programmer and was on the hunt for a CTO for them.

Jack sat with the suggestion for a second, then nodded. "A fresh pair of eyes never hurts."

JIM IS HOLDING COURT AT STARBUCKS

Jim Frost liked holding his meetings at Starbucks. He loved Starbucks. It was the kind of rags-to-riches story any investor would love. Starbucks had started by bringing high quality European- style coffee to one small Pike's Place café and charged three times the going price for a cup. Coffee used to be bottomless and a buck. Now it was single cup of single origin and cost three. Starbucks had invented a market and then owned it. Now there was a Starbucks on every block, and Jim could even enjoy their coffee on an airplane. He wished he'd had a shot at investing in them. And he dreamed of meeting the next Starbucks entrepreneur.

Jim's next appointment came from the coffee bar with espressos in hand, and he rose and gestured them over. The two founders sat down. Dan was a slim young Indian man, Fred a freckled strawberry blond with a Doritos-and-Coke diet waistline.

Jim listened to them talk through their latest change in direction. Their fourth in 18 months. When he had funded them, they were doing diet tracking. Then came gourmet health menus. Now they were focusing on healthy recipes. Jim suppressed a sigh while the entrepreneurs faked excitement about the new direction.

"Our beta users love the site!" Dan gushed. But there was no real excitement in his voice. Fred stared into his espresso as if it were a scrying pool. He didn't even try to meet Jim's eyes. The passion the two had brought to the original idea had foundered on the rocks of a disinterested market. Fred, especially, had loved the technology the tracker had used. Now it was gone, and he was stuck coding a website he didn't care about. He looked tired. And several pounds heavier. Dan was so stuck in hustle mode, he didn't recognize when it was time to turn it off and face their problems honestly.

Some entrepreneurs run out of money. Others run out of heart, Jim thought. These guys are going to do both.

Jim shook their hands, saying goodbye to both the men and his investment. Once a team ran out of heart, there was no reason pouring more money in after it.

When Jim saw Hanna's Civic pull into the parking lot, he wondered about these young entrepreneurs. Would Hanna and Jack be in Dan and Fred's shoes in another couple of quarters? Or would they be Starbucks?

JACK REALLY HATES STARBUCKS

They had to meet at a Starbucks near Jim's office, which always made Jack have small quiet meltdowns inside. The strip mall that held it also sported a Safeway, a Shell Oil, a Taqueria, and a surprisingly good Kaiseki restaurant. Starbucks represented everything Jack found alien and confusing about Silicon Valley. Why did Venture Capitalists always want to meet at Starbucks, when there was better coffee to be had, and much better tea? Why did a Michelin-starred restaurant choose to be in a strip mall? Who needs this much parking? He'd never seen a lot more than half full.

Hanna pulled her aging Civic into a spot in front with ease and was out with her keys in her pocket before the engine had finished shuddering to a halt. Jack followed dutifully.

Seeing Jim cheered him up a bit. Jim sat on the back patio, where he usually held court. Jim was in his late fifties; a former Intel exec who had built two very successful startups, then moved into angel investing. His lined face told more stories of smiling on the sunny golf courses than the stress of all-nighters, though life had handed him more of the latter than the former. He stood, shaking the hands of two young men, both dressed in identical blue dress shirts and khakis. Finishing a pitch up then, Jack thought.

Hanna touched his arm lightly, to hold him back. "I don't feel much like doing the social dance," she muttered. They slowed their walk, and other entrepreneurs left. Jack and Hanna took their seats, greeting Jim. Jack found his seat still warm. They laid out the question of the pivot before Jim.

Jim sat back, and lightly ran his finger along the rim of his double espresso. Every time they met, he was drinking coffee. Yet he never seemed anything but calm, as if he'd stepped out of a yoga class.

"Back when I worked at Intel, we had a story we recalled when facing a hard decision. Back in the eighties, the Japanese were gaining market share in memory. As Intel lost more and more money, there was a ton of internal debate about what to do. Real brutal arguments," Jim said. "One day, Andy Grove and Gordon Moore were talking about it again, and Andy looked out the window at the revolving Ferris wheel of the Great America amusement park in the distance. He turned back to Gordon and asked, 'If we got kicked out and the board brought in a new CEO, what do you think he would do?'. Gordon answered without hesitation, 'He would get us out of memories.' Andy, struck by the clarity of that simple statement said, 'Why shouldn't you and I walk out the door, come back in, and do it ourselves?'

"Well, you know the rest of the story," Jim continued. "That propelled Intel into greater success yet. After that, Intel would always use the revolving door test on really tough decisions. We'd think of what someone not burdened by history and emotion would do." Jim paused, and sipped his espresso.

"So kids, if you were hired as a new CEO, what would you do?"

Jack looked at Hanna, but she remained quiet. He knew what she thought.

Jack said, "I'd have to consider this direction seriously. It's good money. But I'm rather worried if we go this direction, we'll be pressured into lowering quality."

Jim asked, "And then what would happen?"

Jack replied, "I'd have to say no. I'd walk away first." The three of them sat there in silence.

Hanna said, "I'd say no also."

Jack looked up from his untouched tea.

"I don't want to build a company selling a poor product," Hanna said. "That never works in the long run. If I wanted to sell bad tea, I'd work for Bigelow. Or Celestial Seasonings. We're here to change the world, not reproduce it."

Jack looked back into his cup. "I know. Dammit. I know." He'd heard it before; they had talked about it a hundred times. Yet, when it came to money, would she stick to her principles?

Hanna smiled now. "Well, dummy, we are here to get the tea to the people who like to drink it! Not let it grow old and disgusting in the warehouse. Like what you're doing here." She pointed at his cup.

Jack looked at his cup, and back at her, giving her a quick smile. When she talked like this, she reminded him of his sister. Yet Hanna was an MBA. In his department, they'd made fun of MBAs and their weird language: "Exits" and "Maximizing Value." He always figured "value" was their code word for money. But that wasn't what he thought of when he thought of value.

Jack finally spoke. "It seems we've achieved the elusive product/market fit when we weren't paying attention. I suppose if I was the new CEO, I'd have to agree to commit to the pivot."

He saw Hanna's shoulders visibly relax.

"Good," Jim said. "Don't be surprised if you get some resistance from the team. It's typical. I recommend you consider using OKRs to keep things on track." He received blank stares from both the young entrepreneurs. "That stands for Objectives and Key Results. A lot of my companies use them to increase focus and team output. Each quarter set a bold, qualitative Objective and three quantitative Results that let you know when you've hit your Objective.

"So, what do you think a good Objective would be for your group? Something tough, but doable in three months."

"Prove our value to the restaurant suppliers," Hanna quickly replied.

Jack interrupted her, "What do you mean by value?"

"Show we can deliver an excellent product that helps their business."

Jack paused, then nodded. Excellent product. That sounded right.

Jim asked, "How will you know you have succeeded?"

Hanna and Jack went back and forth. Finding a revenue-based Key Result wasn't hard. But agreeing on a metric that would represent the supplier valuing TeaBee was.

"No bargaining?" Jack suggested. "I mean, if it's that good, they won't haggle over cost."

Hanna rolled her eyes at that. "Look Jack, bargaining is just what you do in the business. Your livelihood depends on getting the best price. If my mom wasn't bargaining, I'd check for a pulse. Let's try a retention metric." Jack looked blank. Hanna continued, "Like reorders at 30%?"

Jim jumped in. "OKRs need to be hard goals. The kind you only have a 50/50 shot of achieving. You're trying to get the team to push itself. As your investor, I'd worry if 30% retention was all you're aiming for." This was a sobering reminder that Jim wasn't just a friend; he had skin in the game.

Jack jumped in. "100% reorders!"

Jim smiled. "Is that possible? It can be upsetting to set a goal that the team knows they cannot achieve."

Hanna stepped in. "I think 70% is possible. So far, everyone has re-upped, but that was with my prompting them."

Jack said, "That's something I want to stop if we can. We have a website after all. Surely they can use that to make their orders?"

Hanna replied, "They can't use it. It isn't really set up for their needs."

"Well, we'll put in some OKRs about fixing the site, too, then."

Then Jim's next meeting showed up, and he quietly extracted himself to another table, leaving them to work through the details.

Hanna and Jack discussed goals and metrics until they suddenly realized they were shivering in the shade of the late afternoon. The sun had dipped behind the Starbucks, and their tea was ice cold, but they had real goals they could both live with. They each went home to sleep on it.

HANNA ANNOUNCES THE PIVOT

The next morning in the office, over a pot of Keemun, they reexamined the OKRs they had set the day before. They looked hard, but right.

Hanna and Jack called the team into the conference room. Hanna stood at the front of the room. She still felt awkward addressing a group, even though she'd been forced to do so every week in her entrepreneur class. Their three programmers sat in a row, all with laptops open. Anya, the designer, hid behind a cascade of hair as she drew furiously in a sketchbook. Naoko, the CFO for hire, sat quietly, a hand resting lightly on a pile of printouts of the latest sales. Hanna felt even more nervous, knowing these people were betting their future on Jack and her. No pressure, right?

Hanna took a breath and tried to send it to her toes like her yoga teacher recommended.

"Hey guys." She looked at their faces for encouragement. Well, the faces she could see. Erik, the lead programmer, glanced briefly up from his laptop as she stood, but Cameron and Sheryl, the other two programmers, stayed eyes locked on their code. Jack, sitting next to her, smiled at Hanna and nodded for her to begin.

"We've got an announcement. We're going to make a small, but we believe, significant pivot. We are going to focus solely on selling to restaurant suppliers." She took them through the latest events and through the numbers Naoko had brought with her.

Jack chimed in, "We are still bringing great tea from scrappy producers to fine restaurants. We've just found a more efficient and profitable approach."

Some in the team looked unhappy. Erik was particularly upset. For the first time, he looked up from his computer. "This is bull. This company was started to help farmers and small businesses! That's why I joined."

He was a Midwestern boy, and had come to California to attend Berkeley, but stayed to avoid the Kansas winters.

"These suppliers sell corporate teas. They don't care about the tea farmers! They just care about profit."

Jack replied, "It's good for those growers that they have TeaBee to protect their interests. We'll make sure they get a good price, while reaching new customers."

Hanna chimed in. "Besides, most of them aren't big enough or don't have sufficient consistent supply to interest the restaurant suppliers. When I talked with the restaurants, they were concerned with consistent delivery. When I talked to the restaurant suppliers, they viewed the little guys as too little to be worth the effort until TeaBee aggregated the offering. We can make sure we can always offer a good green and black tea at a minimum."

Jack finished, "Now the tea producers can sell more tea. And, better yet, they can predict how much they are able to sell and know when to hire and or even expand. This could be really great for everyone."

The team seemed to get the change finally, though Hanna noticed Erik had his hand cupped over his mouth, as if to stop himself from commenting. She wondered what was going on in his head.

"Let's discuss what this shift means." Hanna drew a business model canvas on the whiteboard. "We've got a new customer now to consider –the restaurant suppliers. This means some changes. We're going to have to hire some salespeople and a strong customer service department. Our sales have been based on Jack's charm and my foot work." She got a couple laughs there, as everyone knew Jack disliked the sales part of the job. He liked to schmooze, and he often found new clients, but closing the deal, negotiating prices and getting contracts signed: that was all Hanna. "We need people who know what they are doing. Each sale will be in the thousands, not the hundreds. TeaBee is about to be high touch."

Next, they talked through the OKR process, and went through the OKRs.

Hannah led by writing the first OKRs up on the board.

Objective: Establish clear value to restaurant suppliers as a quality tea provider.

KR: Reorders at 70%

KR: 50% of reorders self-serve

KR: Revenue of 250K

Then she added another set of OKRs.

Objective: Build a valuable platform for restaurant suppliers to manage orders.

KR: 80% repeat orders placed online

KR: Satisfaction score of 8/10

KR: Calls reduced 50%

And then she added: "Objective: Build an effective sales team" with KRs on that, and "Objective: Build a responsive customer service approach," and added three more KRs to that goal.

The team discussed if they could hit the goals, and reduced reorders to 60%.

"After all," Erik said, "We can move that number up next quarter, right?"

As the conversation drew to a close, Cameron raised his hand. "But what about our current customers? The restaurants?"

"Oh, we can keep them," said Jack.

Hanna's head spun around. They could?

She opened her mouth to disagree with him, then stopped. They were already introducing so much change to the team. And it wasn't like they were going to go out and sell to new restaurants. She could talk to Jack privately later, perhaps, and form a plan to retire the restaurants gradually. She wasn't avoiding conflict. She was picking her battles. Right?

HANNA ATTENDS A TASTING

Hanna was inputting orders for the distributors when she felt someone standing near her desk. She looked up. Jack stood there, with his coat on, holding several cardboard boxes.

"You about ready?" he asked.

"For what?"

"The tasting? At the XFlight Coworking space? You know? We need to go now, or we'll get clobbered by the traffic."

Hanna stared at him, moving her thoughts from numbers to words. "Look, I need to finish putting in these numbers or Systovore won't get their tea order."

"Why don't they use the site?"

"We talked about this. The site only lets you put in orders in increments of ten. At their size, they'd flip if they had to put in an order 80 times. Either fix the site, or leave me alone to finish this."

"I'll wait in the car."

"It's 95 degrees out there. The car will be an oven!"

"Don't let me die, then." He stalked away with the boxes, muttering to himself. "I hate being late."

Hanna growled, but closed the file she was working on and headed out.

They arrived in plenty of time to set up the tea samples. XFlight was a typical coworking space. It held six small startups of three or four people each in an open loft space. The desks looked Ikea, but the chairs were the usual expensive Herman Millers. It had a central kitchen that held a couple microwaves and a water dispenser. The glassware included branded coffee mugs and Mason jars. "Good thing we brought their own kettles and cups," Jack chirped happily. "No one seems to care about actual quality, just looking hip in this joint."

Hanna felt better, more focused. She had blared disco the entire drive up and was still humming "Car Wash" to herself as she set out the small glass teacups her mom had gotten wholesale. She would do this one tasting, then tell Jack, no more. Jack was loudly socializing with the general manager of the coworking space, running interference for her. A natural introvert, she preferred not to do any more small talk than necessary for survival.

The evening progressed much as others like this had. They had done tastings at coffee shops and a couple bakeries. Jack managed to talk with everyone there, convincing people to try each tea. Hanna and a CEO of a travel app compared notes on angels they had each pitched. The tenants of the space left by 8:00, either back to their desks to code or off to find food. Hanna packed up, tired from interacting with humans and not relishing the drive back. Then she remembered she had one more order to put in. She sighed deeply and put down the box of cups.

"Jack?"

"Hmm?"

"Why did we do this?"

"We just closed an order with the office manager. Fifteen pounds a week! And our brand will be on the packages… that could help recognition."

"Recognition with who? It's not like a restaurant supplier is going to be hanging out in this kitchen. That's our customer."

"Ok, then a VC? Anyhow, we got a sale."

"To a coworking space! It's not our focus!"

"They can self-serve on the website. What's your problem?"

"I'm doing more data entry every day! You are supposed to be running Product. So fix Product!"

"It's in the backlog!"

"Is that engineering for 'go away?'"

"No. Dammit. No." Jack backed off. He looked puzzled, as if confused by her show of anger. But he would be; they never fought. They didn't like fighting. She didn't like fighting, anyhow. She didn't like it now. "Look I'll just cab it home today. That way you get on the road faster." He was offering her a white flag.

Hanna swallowed her distaste of conflict. She had to say something. "No. Jack. Before you call a car, you need to promise me. No more tastings. We agreed on our OKRs. These don't move any of them forward. These are a waste of time."

Jack hesitated. He jammed his hands in his pocket, and then took them out again, as if chided. "These are useful. Networking." His voice was softer now, a hint of doubt entering his voice.

"No. I don't think so. "

And then suddenly, his attitude brightened. "Oh, you are nervous about the sales call with those Monterey blokes. Don't worry! I'll come along! Make sure everyone is chummy! Go! Chill out. Sleep." And he took the box of cups out of her arms and went out the door as her jaw hit the floor. He had completely dismissed her concerns. Chill out? Hanna couldn't chill out. And she certainly couldn't sleep. Not with another order of 20 different teas to type in.

JACK COMMITS TO QUALITY

Jack got into the office by late morning. He slowly locked his bike to a rack in the back. Hanna was an early bird, and Jack didn't feel like rehashing last night's fight. She'd apologize and he'd feel bad, or he'd apologize, and what if she didn't forgive him? Anyway, he was going to feel bad. He just wanted to run a good company that made a good product.

He'd seen so many of his favorite product designs get ruined over time. Even his beloved smart phone was now big and clunky in his pocket, when it used to be a joy to hold. When he'd worked over the summer for a company he'd always admired, he saw how Product Managers and the businesspeople threw over quality for quick returns. Then he realized why everything got worse: money. The business folks pushed to get an uptick by end of quarter so they could bag a bonus. No worry for customer experience or the reputation of the company! He decided then that the only way to assure quality and stay true to a vision was for him to start a company himself. Now he worried he'd get pushed into becoming one of them, those executives he'd resented, and give up his principles to keep TeaBee going.

Perhaps if he just explained to Hanna why showing off their product quality at these tastings was so important. One needs a strong brand for strong word of mouth, and strong word of mouth meant getting tea into people's mouths! Then people would understand how good TeaBee was, and the money would sort itself out. That's what he'd do; he'd just explain it. She'd understand; she loved tea, too.

When he walked in, he noticed her chair was empty. That meant she was out selling. His shoulders relaxed. He hadn't even realized he was holding them tightly in. Well, conversation for another day. He headed over to his desk, but before he could sit, Erik waved him over.

"Hey man, I saw something cool, and I stayed up doing a prototype. Check it."

Erik sat back in his chair, his long legs sprawling beneath the desk. He gestured toward the monitor with his slim yellowed fingers. Jack briefly wondered how many cigarettes he smoked a day.

Erik scrolled down the front page of the site. The navigation stayed put, while the rest moved. Then he kicked off the order form, which showed each field as soon as the last was correctly filled out.

"Pretty slick," said Jack, admiring the effects.

Erik shrugged. "Just killing time while waiting on the bulk order spec."

Jack stomach tightened. "That would be on me. I'm about half there, but I had to stop for a bit. I was prepping for the tea tasting."

"Dude, don't sweat it!" Erik said. "Seriously. Those restaurant suppliers should suck it up and type in their orders. Their making enough money from ripping off farmers. Let them spend a little, create a data entry job at least."

The phrase "data entry" made Jack feel worse. "Hanna's been typing it in, not the suppliers." She'd been doing the work because he hadn't written up a technical spec so Erik could code the new functionality.

Erik seemed oblivious of Jack's stress. "Anyhow, I don't get it. Why are we making the middleman fatter? Wasn't the point to help the farmers? And the restaurants? You know, the indies?"

Jack liked meeting with restaurants. He liked doing the coworking spaces and the incubators. He did not much care for the corporate offices most of the suppliers had.

"I think Hanna wants to be the next Starbucks, sometimes," Erik finished up his rant.

"Yeah, I dunno," Jack finally replied "Seems like every time we meet up with an investor it's at Starbucks. That's what they want. The giant exit, the big return."

Erik nodded. "Well, good thing we're watching out for the tea growers. Somebody's got to."

"Yeah, mate. Right. The world has enough mass-produced garbage. We've got to show people what quality looks like!"

"Dude. Exactly."

Jack returned to his desk feeling better. They had good tea, the packaging designs were looking good, the website was solid. Hanna'd come around.

HANNA TALKS NUMBERS

It was late into the afternoon when Hanna finally returned. Sunlight streamed past the flip charts an engineer had taped to the window to try to reduce the light.

She walked up to Jack, not even pausing to set her bag down at her desk. "Let's talk."

She walked to the conference room.

"We need the room, Erik," she said as she entered. Her tone brooked no argument.

He unfolded himself from the chair and carried his laptop back to his desk.

Hanna sat down. Jack sat across from her, keeping the big table between them. On the wall were the OKRs posters he'd made at the beginning of the quarter. He wondered idly how many they'd reached so far.

Hanna leaned forward. "Jack, you extended Anya's contract."

He blinked. "Yup. We aren't done."

"We can't afford her. We can't afford us! We are six weeks into the quarter. In a few months, we're going to have to go out and try to raise money again. But our numbers are not moving. I don't think anyone is going to invest."

Jack continued to stare at Hanna uncomprehendingly. He seemed unprepared for this conversation.

Hanna glared at him. "Do you look at the dashboards I send you? Jack!"

"Um, I'm not really a number kind of guy. But we closed XFlight! And the restaurant last week!"

"And we lost a restaurant the week before. They went under. They do that. We are revenue neutral. Look, we discussed this. We need the suppliers. Just two more this quarter, and five next. And we'll have strong numbers, strong enough to start fundraising."

"Can't we just get a bunch of restaurants?"

Hanna stared, speechless. She saw the moment Jack must have realized that they had had this conversation just two months before. But it was too late. She exploded. "We can't close enough restaurants in time. Not without hiring a lot of salespeople, and that will increase our burn rate. Restaurants are slow and cautious and take forever to close. And when we do close them, they order only a pound of tea a week. One supplier is worth 100 restaurants."

Hanna burned with fury. "Jack, your refusal to pay attention to basic economics is driving me crazy. If you were a designer in some big company, maybe you could nap during the math part of the meetings, but for heaven's sake, this is your company!" Which wasn't going to be his for long if they went under. She slammed her hand on the table, causing it to shudder. Jack took a step back.

Hanna shook her head, frightened by her outburst, and sat down. She took a deep breath, and continued, her voice low now, and more disturbing for the new calm it held.

"Jack, if we can't raise money, we'll have to let people go. You know my mom's restaurant? It wasn't her first. My grandparents had a restaurant before she did. That's where she learned how to run a place and fell in love with the business. But during the economic downturn in the seventies, no one ate out. My grandparents tried to keep the place open, and they tried to keep the staff on. They didn't want anyone to not have a job when things were so tough. But things didn't get better fast enough. And the whole place went under. Maybe if they'd fired someone sooner and found a way to cut back..." Hanna leaned back in her wobbly Ikea chair.

She looked at Jack, showing none of the emotion she felt so keenly. "I can't make that mistake."

"What are you saying?" Jack asked softly. He looked concerned, maybe even a little afraid.

"I'm asking you to commit. Jack, what do you want from this?" She gestured around the room, covered with OKR posters, smiling customer personas and website mockups. Jack's work on the company surrounded them.

"I guess I wanted a place to do things right. I wanted to find something wonderful, and find a way to help other people fall in love with it the way I love it. And I thought it would be fun."

He paused and leaned forward, elbows on the table, hands clasped in front of him. "And I thought it would be fulfilling. Every day I read the tech news and see people making things that change the world. I want to be part of that."

"Sometimes it is fun," Hanna continued. "But you can't do the fun part and leave the hard part to other people all the time. If we get this wrong, we will go under. And people will lose jobs. And no one will find out how great tea can be." She managed a grin that was only half a grimace.

Jack replied, "I'll go through the dashboards, ok?"

Hanna nodded. Jack sighed deeply, and Hanna wondered if he just wanted the conversation to end, or if he really planned to change.

JACK EAVESDROPS

Jack sat at his computer with his headphones on. He had been listening to music, but it had stopped some time ago. He stared at Hanna's dashboard. What were these numbers? She had the OKRs, but where did they change? How much were they making? What did they have left? Nothing looked familiar, but he was embarrassed to ask. Anyhow, Hanna was out on a sales call until four. Maybe he'd suck it up and ask to have it explained if he hadn't figured it out by then. He figured if he just stayed with it, the numbers should eventually reveal themselves to him.

Through the headphones, he heard the murmurs of Sheryl and Erik. He assumed they were discussing some bug triage, but then he caught a few words. "Hanna." "Sell out." He couldn't help but tune in to their conversation.

"Yeah, typical MBA bull," he heard Erik say. "She just wants to make money."

"Maybe," said Sheryl. Sheryl was not a talker.

"Look. She's got us in the pockets of the big companies. She's probably setting up the company to flip. That's what they teach them in 'B-School.'"

Erik made scare quotes with his fingers around "B-School." Jack tried to hide that he was watching from the corner of his eyes. Yeah, he thought, an MBA doesn't teach you everything.

Erik continued, "Those people just drive revenues up, then they fire everyone to make a better bottom line. So they can get the biggest exit, see?"

That didn't sound quite so plausible to Jack any more. That wasn't Hanna's story.

Then he heard Erik say something that chilled him to his bones.

"They won't be getting me with any 'cost cutting measures.' I still haven't gotten the spec, so I've been making a few adjustments to the code in my free time. Good luck to any new CTO they want to hire. He won't be able to figure anything out."

Jack had heard stories of engineers who wrote confusing code so they could never be fired. He always thought it was a Silicon Valley legend. A kind of engineering boogie man. He was wrong. He closed the dashboard, and opened the spec. Then he reopened the dashboard in his second monitor. And he sat like that, eyes flicking back and forth between them, trying to figure out what to do.

JACK GETS MORE NEWS

The office phone rang. It rang so rarely, Jack jumped. Hanna picked it up, coolly answering "Hello, TeaBee, Hanna speaking." She paused, then continued, "Yes, fine, Philip!"

It was one of the restaurant suppliers! Jack sat at the edge of his seat. Maybe he could get her to ask for a testimonial to help with sales on the site. He hovered, in case there was a pause.

"I'm so sorry!" Hanna replied, her brow furrowing.

So much for a testimonial, Jack thought.

"Look, can we make it up to you? I can drive over the tea!"

Now a long break as she listened.

"I understand. Again, I am so sorry. Goodbye."

She hung up, and Jack walked over to her. Hanna let her forehead fall to her keyboard.

Jack waited to be noticed. He understood what it cost to be interrupted.

She looked up at him. "We lost Jefferson."

"What?"

"Too many wrong orders."

Jack noticed she was wringing her hands, tangling her fingers together and apart over and over.

"How is the bulk order flow coming, Jack?" she asked. "I can't keep doing the order entry."

"Um, I handed it to Erik yesterday. I figured he should have something to do."

"Yeah. He should." Hanna looked at him, her eyes going cold and empty. Her hands lay still in her lap now.

"Ok, you can call Tenzo Farms."

"What?"

"You can tell them that we won't have any orders for them. Jefferson was the only one taking Matcha. They have most of Japantown. Tell Tenzo they are losing their biggest customer and hope they haven't hired anyone lately to help with the increased orders."

Jack paled.

Hanna turned away from him. "Go," she said. "Go do it, Mr. President."

HANNA GETS ADVICE

Hanna stood outside the Starbucks, hesitating. She wasn't sure if Jim was the right person to go to for advice. But she didn't know who else to talk to. Losing Jefferson had shaken her, shaken her faith in herself. Jack couldn't help; *he* was the problem.

She bought two espressos and joined Jim on the back patio. He stood and smiled as she handed him one of the cups. "Where's Jack today?"

Hanna hesitated, and then said, "I wanted to speak to you privately."

Jim's smile disappeared. His next words were kind enough, but he's eyes flicked over her, assessing. "So what's on your mind, kiddo?"

Hanna continued, nervously. "Well, we've got some challenges. I was hoping for some advice."

Jim gestured to go ahead.

"It's Jack." She took Jim through her litany of complaints. "And because of his insistence on farting around with these tastings and the packaging, instead of handling the technical issues we have, we've lost Jefferson."

She looked at Jim to respond, and it was as if the laugh-lines around his eyes had been erased. His lips pursed slightly, then he laid both hands flat on the table. "He has to step into his role. Have you explained that to him?"

"Yes." Then she thought a second. "Maybe? I pointed out he was wasting his time." But she only mocked him about being President. That was not the same. "I think he knows."

"Hanna, it's not complicated. Tell him clearly. Then tell him again. When you are tired of saying it, people are starting to hear it. You've got to focus on the Objectives and Results, and you have to make sure he knows *his* role in getting there." He sipped the last of his espresso. "Know your role as well. Your job as CEO is to set the goals and have the hard conversations. Go be CEO."

"I'm worried about the next round." Hanna wanted so badly for Jim to tell her what to do.

Jim shrugged. "Push comes to shove, we can get in a more seasoned exec."

Hanna froze. Her stomach leapt into her mouth and the espresso burned the back of her throat. She briefly wished she'd stuck with the bad tea she usually got.

"I like you both personally, so I'm going to be honest. You've just told me you are falling apart. I'm your investor, not your mom. You get it together with Jack, or you remove him. You focus on fixing your numbers. Or I look for a way to get someone in to get the company to the next level. It's not complicated. You've got the beginning of something, but the Valley is littered with the beginnings of good things."

It was not uncommon. She'd heard stories. Founders replaced with experienced executives forced upon them by their investors.

"I'll get there. I mean I'll talk to Jack." The espresso was making her heart race.

"Good. I look forward to our next check in."

HANNA GETS MORE BAD NEWS

When Hanna got in, it was late. Jack still sat in front of his computer. The office was otherwise empty. Everyone else had gone home, unless Erik was lurking about in a conference room. She put down her coat, and was about to sit down when Jack strode across the room toward her.

"What's up?" she asked. She wasn't ready to have "the talk" yet. She wanted to put together a game plan.

"We need to talk."

Hanna looked down, hoping to stall. "Now? I've got more orders to enter."

"I think Erik is sabotaging us."

"Is he…" She looked at the conference room.

"No"

"That's crazy. Why?"

"I overheard him. He told Sheryl he was obfuscating the code for job security reasons."

Hanna sat down heavily, on top of her bag. She then stood, removed it and sat down again. Jack perched at the edge of her desk.

"Jack…"

"I know."

He didn't know, not by half. "We need a CTO. Soon. Neither of us knows enough code to know if this is true." Her entire company was unraveling before her eyes.

"It's not about code. It's about Erik. I knew he wasn't behind the pivot, but this is over the top. He's gossiping." Jack swallowed hard. "He's saying nasty things about you."

"We should fire him. Can we fire him?"

"I don't know."

Hanna opened her laptop, hands shaking slightly. Too much caffeine she thought. "So, did you call Tenzo?"

"I think we need to focus on Erik right now."

She knew then he hadn't.

"I… I need to think. Let's sit down tomorrow. I need to digest this."

She felt utterly alone.

JACK MAKES A CALL

Jack spent the morning not calling Tenzo Farms. He'd never delivered bad news before. He'd never fired anyone. He'd never even told a client off, though he had wanted to many times.

He spent his afternoon not calling them either. He knew he'd either have to call them by six, before they went home, or first thing in the morning. Hanna would be in his face tomorrow. He left his desk and headed to the Bayshore Trail.

Their little office was off the frontage road of Highway 101, in the swath of land between the road and the Bayshore Park. It was populated with a variety of startups, consulting companies and odd businesses, from animal hospitals to educational services. A large bookkeeping company anchored one end, a tiny airport enjoyed by fresh-minted millionaires at the other.

Everyone walked the bay when they got stuck on a hard problem. Hanna liked to have her one-on-ones walking on the trail, unless there was a confidential matter. He missed their walks here. It seemed like every time they talked these days it was confidential. But here was nature, a good antidote to days of humming screens.

He had thought that having a startup was a good idea. Designers pretty much never found startups, it seemed like. They were scared of the money thing. Now he wondered if they were really afraid of being in charge. He'd taken a year off between college and grad school, and done a bunch of consulting. It was easy: make the client happy. Now it was confusing. Who was the client? And no one was ever going to be happy.

He'd tried calling Jefferson to talk them into a second chance. That went over like a lead balloon. They were done. They'd told Hanna they were done, and they seemed annoyed by having to tell him the same thing. Jack worried Hanna might bust him for wrecking a chance to close them later.

In the end, he decided to do the call to Tenzo from his cell, on a bench, looking at the salt flats.

He dialed the number.

"Hi, this is Jack from TeaBee. May I speak with Atushi?"

"Hey! It's me. How are you doing? How are things in startup land?"

"Hey. Um, well, not great."

"Ok. What's up?"

"Well. I have some bad news. Jefferson has stopped working with us. We are not going to have any more orders for Matcha after the 17th."

Silence on the end of the phone. "Are you still there?" Jack asked.

"I'm here," Atushi answered. "I just don't know what to say. Can we fix it? Was it a quality thing?"

"No. It was..." Jack felt bile rise in his throat. "It was us. We ballsed up an order, and they cut us off. I'm sorry."

"Ok. Got it. So we'll have to adjust next month's...we have a really good guy who was working part-time. We were talking about converting him." Jack heard Atushi's disappointment. "...but now... sorry, that's my business. Thanks for letting us know quickly.

Appreciate it." Atushi's voice was now firm, but not angry. Jack heard the pain though. A small business was always teetering, he had learned. He was the one who had given it a nudge in the wrong direction today.

"Sorry, mate." Jack had nothing else he could say. He looked for some bit of cheer to offer but came up empty. "I'm sorry."

"Yeah. Me, too." Atushi sighed. "Talk later." And he hung up, not waiting for Jack's response.

Jack sat for a while. A heron landed in the small creek, a beautiful explosion of white wings on blue water. Jack found no comfort in it.

That was it, he decided. He couldn't just focus on product. He had to design the entire business. He had to understand the whole thing, and make sure every choice was the right one. For the first time, he realized TeaBee wasn't just deliciousness in a good- looking box. It was the people he worked with and the conversations they had. It was the plans they made together. It was even the damn numbers. His business was an ecosystem, and he was more a gardener than designer. He had to get better at his job.

He stood, jammed his fists in his hoodie pockets, and walked back to the office.

OUT OF TIME

The call with Tenzo Farms lit a fire under Jack. For about a week. Hanna kept typing in orders, and got the front-end dev, Cameron, to double check them before she committed them. It was a slower process than before, but they couldn't afford to lose another supplier. Cameron didn't seem to mind. He sat next to her and flirted as he looked over the numbers. Hanna wasn't sure how she felt about that, but decided it was far from her biggest problem right now and ignored him.

Hanna left Cameron double checking the orders, running his finger along her monitor as he tracked each line carefully. She approached Jack, sitting at his computer "So, we're launching bulk order flow this week?"

"Yes, yes. I am just changing a couple things after usability testing."

"The best is the enemy of the good," Hanna muttered.

"Huh?" Jack grunted, head down.

"Never mind. Just launch. I'll buy some Nukey Brown for the launch party." Newcastle was his favorite. Pricey, but it made him happy. Anything to get the damn thing out.

"We've got a tasting at Daily Bread tonight," Jack mentioned hesitantly.

"You are kidding me."

"Sorry, it was set up months ago!"

Hanna's eyes wandered to the OKR poster. Damn, it had grown invisible in the weeks it had been up. The next step now stared at her: "Hire three salespeople."

She turned back to Jack. "You have a tasting to run. I have Objectives to hit. Good luck with that."

She scooted back to her desk to get a job posting up. She paused again, trying to decide when to talk to him about what she learned from Jim. But maybe he was getting better on his own?

And quite suddenly, the end of the quarter arrived.

NUMBERS

Hanna pulled Jack into the conference room again to review at their OKRs. Again they kicked out Erik, who bragged, "I've shaved .500 seconds off the load time of the homepage!" When Jack told him to "sod off" this time, it was considerably less friendly.

Hanna laid out the printouts of their OKRs on the table and pulled out a red pen to circle misses. They looked at the reddening sheets of paper.

"Sales team?" asked Jack

"Frank's great, but he's one guy. I didn't get the ad up until halfway through the quarter." She pointed at *50% of reorders self-serve.* "And this?"

"You know. We launched the new bulk order system last week."

"Yeah, I've got the usage numbers somewhere." She shuffled the papers around. "Ok. Hmm, 15% so far."

"Well it was new. I didn't want to piss off any of the customers. So I just told a couple restaurants and one of the suppliers about it."

Hanna let out a long shuddering sigh. "I suppose that's right. I just wish we'd gotten it out sooner."

She paused, gathering her thoughts. "Have you got that satisfaction survey you ran last week? Did we get enough results to get a read?"

Jack pulled out a colorful printout of a survey with one hand, while chewing at the skin around his thumbnail. "Um, yes, I think it's enough responses. The results are.... they are.... uneven, I think I'd say."

"So, not that KR."

"No." Jack looked chagrined. Customer experience was *his* baby.

She pulled out the sales numbers. "I've been watching this one." She pointed to revenue. "Close, but not close enough. There was a little uptick here and I thought we had it." She pointed to the end of month two. "But then Jefferson..."

The pain of the loss of Jefferson sat between them like a poisonous toad. They stared at the chart.

"So," Jack said. "Zero?"

"Zero." Hanna said. "We made zero OKRs." The weight of the red ink made her exhausted and angry. "This is bullshit," she yelled, "How did we not make any of the OKRs? I mean, I know we were supposed to make them hard, but it's like nobody even tried!"

It's like I didn't try, a voice in her head said.

It's like Jack didn't try, said another.

"Hey, we got the new branding system up!" Jack replied. "And we've been helping the restaurants with the website. We improved the checkout flow for them. But..." his voice trailed off. "None of those things were things we agreed to focus on." He put his hands in his hoodie pockets, looking down at the papers in front of him. They both knew nothing *he* did was there.

Hanna stood looking at him, lips tightly pressed together. Then she turned on her heel and strode out of the conference room. She had to get out of that room. Only bad things happened there.

Jack chased her. "You can't walk out of this. We need to finish." He spoke in a low tone. The office was still full.

"Why? It's clear enough. We fucked up." Tears lurked behind her eyes. She had to stay angry or it was going to get embarrassing. "My mom always said, 'In times of crises people go back to the thing that made them successful. Even when it's not the right thing to do.'" Hanna knew she and Jack were both scared, leading a company for the first time. "You focused on design and usability for the old customers. And I went out and sold, instead of building a team who could do it." Her voice rose, cracking with emotion. "And now we don't have numbers that justify investment. I don't think we can turn it around."

Suddenly she noticed the office had grown silent. Filled with embarrassed horror, she headed toward the front door, to escape to the bay.

Jack's cell phone vibrated in his pocket. He glanced at the display: Jim.

"Hanna, hold on!" he shouted, then answered. "Jim," he mouthed, pointing at the phone.

"Jack? Jim. Can you kids swing by the Starbucks? I am talking to a fellow here, and I think you ought to meet."

"Be right over! Fifteen minutes!" he said brightly.

Hanna glowered. "Great. Great. I am not ready to have this conversation. We didn't hit our numbers." Her voice rose again. Jack's cheeks now flushed with embarrassment, but she didn't lower her voice. She was too angry. "What are we going to tell him?"

"So the OKRs didn't work. I mean, it's hardly our fault. It's his system, we did it, and it didn't do anything. It's just another Silicon Valley fad."

"Jack, do you honestly think it was the OKRs fault?" Hanna hissed.

"I can't say. It's a system that's supposed to help us kick arse. And we didn't kick anything."

Hanna lowered her voice. Her anger had become a deadly calm. "Something certainly didn't work."

She grabbed her jacket with the car keys and strode out the door. Jack followed, all eyes in the open office watching as their founders stormed out the door.

HANNA AND JACK MEET A NEW PLAYER

The drive to Starbucks felt too short. Hanna realized halfway there the car was silent; she had not even thought to plug in her music. Jack stared out the window, away from her.

Hanna slid her Civic into a tight space between two minivans, and Jack sucked in his breath to slide out of the passenger side. But he didn't complain as he usually did about giant American cars.

As they approached the back patio, they saw Jim sitting across from a dark-haired man in his late twenties, draped across the chair like he owned the place. He had close-cropped hair, dark aviator sunglasses, and a tattoo peeked out of his black T-shirt. As they got closer, they saw the T-shirt was of a My Little Pony version of Dr. Who, and the tattoo was the RSA-perl program. His nerd credentials were fully in order.

Who was it, Hanna wondered? Another seed investor? He'd never invest once they confessed their failure.

Jim waved toward the empty seats at the table. "Hello folks! I may have found your CTO."

"No pressure," the alpha geek grinned.

So this wasn't to be a numbers review, Hanna thought as she sat down. Her stomach unknotted slightly.

Jim introduced his guest. "This is Raphael. He just left S.O.S."

"The game company?" Jack asked.

"Yup," said Raphael.

"Congrats on the IPO," said Jack.

"It was ok." His grin widened, telling another story.

Jim made up for Raphael's lack of chattiness. "Before that, he was at a startup that was bought by Google."

"Aqui-hire. And I worked on Orkut, so…." He shrugged. Getting your company bought for the talent was still a respectable exit, and landing at Orkut, Google's first experiment at social network, was hardly embarrassing.

"So why aren't you on a beach somewhere?" Jack asked.

"I'm not done. Games are great. I had some juicy problems. But I want to do more."

Hanna took a look at Jack. Jack sat upright, listening intently.

Raphael went on, "I've been reading about the single original coffee that high-end coffee shops offer. It's allowing coffee growers to sell directly to roasters, at a much better price. It's improving lives in coffee-growing countries. I don't see why it couldn't be done for other markets!"

He paused and drank from his cup. "Jim has been telling me what you've already done, and I think this could make a difference in a lot of lives."

Jack began to throw off his doldrums. "Exactly… instead of paying low prices for tea, and blending good and bad into mediocre, we can bring great tea to everyone!"

Raphael cocked his head. "Why does that matter to you?"

"I care about quality," Jack said. "I can't stand badly made things. My mum, she loved bargains. She'd buy anything as long as it was on sale. I had 20 pairs of jeans, none I could be seen in out of the house. And one pair of 501's, which I wore every day. If you can experience something well made, well designed, you know the difference. I know we can do that here."

Hanna had never asked herself why Jack was such a perfectionist. She'd just written it off as a designerly quirk. Now she saw he was on a mission as well. It just wasn't the same as hers. Maybe if she could get Raphael to join, she'd have someone sensible to partner with.

Maybe she could close the deal by sharing her passion.

She jumped in. "Plus, think of the people whose lives we'll change. For example, Wakamatsu Farms was founded by the first Japanese immigrants in California. It's now a cultural heritage site that has just started producing tea again. We'll be able to place that tea in restaurants to help raise money for restoration of their lands. And there is a family farm in Hawaii I was chatting with this morning who would love to be able to get their tea to more people. We can do that, if we can succeed."

"That's exactly what I mean!" Raphael pounded his fists on the table so that the cardboard cups shook. "Work that raises the bar! Work that makes the world better by giving entrepreneurs a way to compete against industry."

Hanna felt excited, and yet… she also felt she was selling a lie. There was no way she could let him join without talking about their OKRs. And Jim should know, too. Better she bring it up than wait until he asked. She slid her hands under the table so she could turn her rings, fidgeting privately.

"There is something we should talk about, before we go any further. We set several critical goals last quarter, and we met none of them."

Jack shot her a look like she had just betrayed them. Maybe she had, but she couldn't bring Raphael in under false pretenses.

"We set five Objectives, one around value, one around providing a platform, one around sales and…" She trailed off. She couldn't remember the other two. She looked to Jack. He shrugged. Well, it hardly mattered now. "We gave them all Key Results in the form of hard metrics. And we did not make any." She took a long breath, looking around the table, then back to Raphael. "I understand if that might make you think twice about joining us."

To their surprise, Raphael, chimed in, cheerful as ever. "You're doing it wrong," he said. "No, seriously, I used them at my last two jobs. They work, totally. But five OKRs? You can't even remember them all. How can your team? Carvil, the dude who ran the Clinton campaign, had a hard time keeping Clinton from doing his policy wonk thing. Every time he got on stage, he wanted to talk about education, foreign policy, energy, all that. And Carvil said, 'If you say three things, you say nothing.' You know, keep it simple stupid. It's the economy, stupid. Focus on one key message. Same things with OKRs. Plus your weekly check ins go on forever if you have that many Objectives!"

"*Weekly* check ins?" Jack queried. "We try to stay pretty meeting free at TeaBee."

Raphael shook his head. "I get it, but you can't just set goals up and hope they happen. You have to execute against them as a team. That means check ins. Just like the daily stand-ups and weekly planning we do in Agile. It can be a good, useful meeting if you have a framework you use every week to guide the meeting." He grabbed a napkin and unfolded it on the table. The creases divided the napkin into four quadrants.

He dug a Sharpie out of his laptop bag, and wrote: "Objective," followed by three "Key Results." He then wrote "5/10" after each KR.

"Okay, so you got that the Objective is the inspiration for the quarter, yeah? And the Results are what happens if you do the right things. It's easy to forget them, though, because every day something cool shows up. So every Monday you look at them. And you ask, are we closer or farther from making these Results? We used a confidence rating at S.O.S. We'd start the quarter with each Key Results at five out of ten."

"Fifty percent confidence? A 50/50 shot at making it?" asked Hanna.

"Exactly. Goals aren't divided into regular and stretch goals. They're all stretch goals. And they need to be hard. Not impossible, just hard. Impossible goals are depressing. Hard goals are inspiring." Raphael looked around the table. Hanna was now leaning forward, and Jack back, the opposite of a few moments before. He continued. "So each week, you have a conversation. You say, have we gone up or down? If you are dropping to 2/10 from 8/10, you want to know why. What changed? Helps you learn as well as track."

Jack spoke up, "No way, mate. We've got tons to track. We can't just ignore our other metrics."

"I have to agree with Jack here. We can't just stop paying attention to everything," Hanna agreed.

Raphael shook his head. He moved his pen to the lower right and wrote "Health."

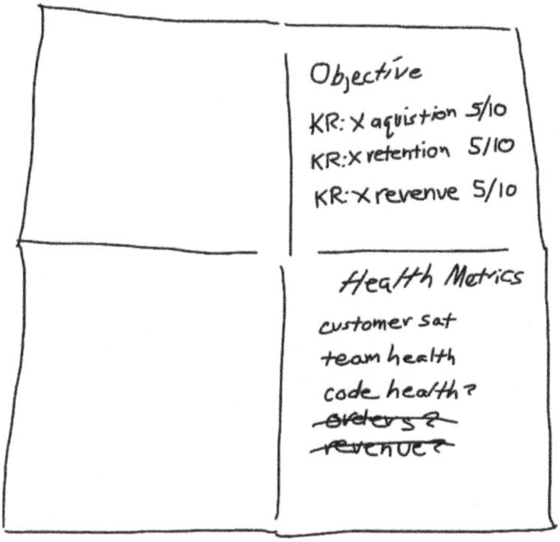

"Hang on. Here, in the lower right, we put health metrics. These are things we want to protect while we shoot for the moon up here." He pointed to the OKRs.

Hanna and Jack glanced at each other, checking to see if the other was also confused. Raphael took a deep breath.

"Let me explain. Let's say we pick an Objective that's about radical pipeline growth. We're trying to get as many suppliers and distributors partnering with us as we can, right?"

The founders nodded in unison.

"Well, we don't want to forget our current customers in the rush to get new ones. So maybe we do this."

He wrote: "Customer Satisfaction: Green" in the lower right. "This way we force a discussion each week about whether our customers are still happy. Lots of stuff can go here."

He wrote "team health, code health, orders, revenue" in a list. "But just like with the OKRs, we want focus. So we'll pick a couple to talk about each week with the entire company, and we can review the rest less often, just us chickens."

"Customer satisfaction is a must," said Jack. "Maybe code health? We don't want bad code."

"Bad code can become a problem easily," Raphael agreed.

"No, look, guys," Hanna interjected. "Code is code, but we are more a relationship business than a tech company. Let's get real. I like the Objective to be around sales, but health of the team, or better yet the bottom line, really seems more important."

Raphael replied, "OKRs are the thing you want to push, the *one* thing you want to focus on making better. The health metrics are the key things to continue to watch. Making them the same doesn't make a lot of sense."

"What about customer satisfaction and team health?" Jack questioned. "We don't want to burn people out."

"I wouldn't mind people working a bit more," replied Hanna.

"You don't need people to work more, you need people to work on the right things," Raphael replied.

"Let's focus on that first. Let's put down customer satisfaction and team health and sit with that for now. So now we have goals on the right, what we want to push on and what we want to protect."

He moved to the left side of the napkin, and wrote "P1" three times, and "P2" twice.

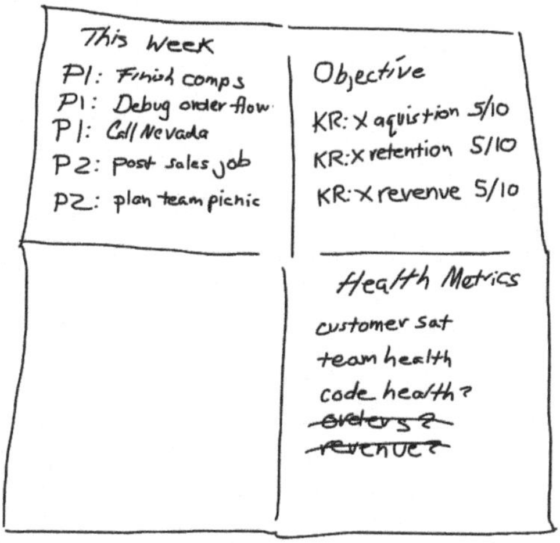

"Here you write the three to five big things you will do this week to affect the OKRs. You share them, so you," he nodded to Hanna, "can question if we are spending time on the things that will get us our Results."

"Hey, I do more than three things a week," Jack complained.

"This isn't some contest to show who does the most busy work," Raphael replied. "You don't list everything you do. You list the things that must happen or you're not going to make your Objectives. Life always gives you plenty to do. The secret is not forgetting the things that matter."

"Yes, yes, yes. What's in the last slot?" Hanna asked, pointing at the lower left. She felt renewed and inspired.

"I call that 'heads up.' It's the pipeline of important things you expect to happen in the next month. That way Marketing, Engineering, Sales and all don't get caught flat footed when something has to be supported."

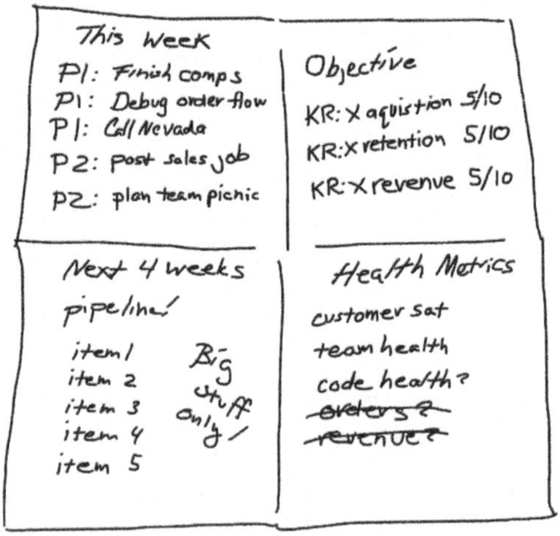

"So we go through this all every week?" Hanna asked.

"Yep."

"And we talk about each point? I can call out folks who are doing things that don't meet our goals?"

"That's your job."

"I think this might work." She bit her lower lip thoughtfully. "I really think this just might work."

They made plans to have Raphael join them Monday as interim CTO, so he could try on the company and so they could try him out as well. But Hanna felt it was a done deal. He was their perfect technical cofounder. She felt a bit less alone.

THE EXECUTIVE TEAM

The Sunday before Raphael started, he met with Hanna and Jack met at the Palo Alto Café. The little coffee shop was mostly empty at this early hour. While Starbucks and Philz had lines out the door with commuters filling up, the PAC's first customers were the TeaBee team and a dad watching his toddler climb under the secondhand wooden tables that furnished the place.

Hanna and Jack were rabidly loyal to the PAC. It was one of the few coffee shops in town that really cared about tea and had been TeaBee's first customer. It was typically quiet until ten, when families, retired gentlemen playing dice and writers would settle in to while away the long hours of the day. It was one of the last few cafés free of entrepreneurs and VCs pitching each other.

The newly bonded executive team began planning.

"Shall we introduce Raph here at the team meet?" asked Jack, casually truncating Raphael's name.

"No one likes to be surprised. Let's introduce him to them one at a time, before the meeting," Hanna replied.

"Yep. That's what I've seen before. Plus, you want to send an email announcement tonight," Raphael added.

And then Jack looked at Hanna, raising an eyebrow. "Erik?"

She thrust out her chin. "Go for it."

Jack ground his molars together, then spat out what they were both thinking about. "Raphael. There is a guy on the team. He's… well, he's been fucking with the code. Obfuscating it. So other people can't work on it."

"Fire him," Raphael replied.

"Well, we thought… I mean… you are the CTO now. You could look and see, then fire him if you can."

"Nope. You hired him, you fire him. I'll deal with whatever has to be dealt with after."

"But aren't you worried?"

"It's not a complicated system. If I need to, I'll rewrite it. But you cannot let a bad apple stay put. They poison everything, like the saying. You need to fire him and you need to do so by end of day tomorrow. Then walk him out. If he's done what you've said, you can't let him near his computer once he's let go."

Hanna looked at Jack. "You're head of Product."

Jack looked at Hanna. "You are CEO."

Hanna paused, sipped her extremely excellent tea. She thought about her mother, and her grandparents. She thought about Tenzo and the other tea producers.

Then she said, "Damn right. He's gone." She took another pause and looked at Jack. "And if things don't change, you are next."

Jack wasn't sure she was kidding.

His first Monday, Raphael came in at eight. Hanna sat typing away at her desk. She gestured vaguely at him and went back to typing. Soon she smelled coffee, and she smiled. He'd found the stash Cameron kept in the freezer.

At ten, with the office full, Erik strode in. Hanna stopped typing. Showtime, she thought. She nodded to Raph, who was camped next to her on an empty desk. They got up and walked Raphael over to the engineering pod to introduce him to his new team.

"Is that coffee I smell?" Erik asked, accusingly.

"Not everyone can start their day with tea." Raph smiled.

"Don't I know it!" replied Cameron.

Erik frowned, his first insult having missed its mark. "Look, I get you've built some big name games. But I gotta warn you, tea might look simple, but it's not. We've rolled our own system for order management here. It's hard to handle the rapidly fluctuating supply, but I've got an algo that predicts it."

"Good to hear," Raph replied.

"You are familiar with algorithm design?"

"I'm ok. I worked on search at my last two companies."

Hanna interrupted the interrogation, "Erik, can I talk to you about an issue in the conference room? Before we start the meeting?" she asked.

"Um, I just want to do a few more things."

"Now," Hanna insisted.

He shrugged and reached for his laptop.

She placed her hand lightly on the docked machine. "We don't need that."

Erik rolled his eyes with a "whatever" expression and followed her into the conference room.

Hanna sat, gesturing for Erik to do the same. Erik stayed standing.

"Erik, we know what you've been doing with the code. That's not acceptable here."

Erik jammed his hands in his jeans pockets. Hanna waited. She struggled not to say anything into the silence. She counted the seconds, keeping silent. He opened his mouth, but it seemed an eternity before he said anything. As if he was fitting words on his tongue until he found the ones that felt right.

"What you are doing with the company is not acceptable!" Erik spat out. "This is not the company I joined!"

Hanna began to prepare her next words. Before she could say anything, though, Erik started back in.

"Fucking gamer guy? What is that? Prepping for an IPO? You bring him just so you can raise another round? Do you care about the farmers? Do you care about people?"

Hanna was aghast. What could he be talking about? They were years from any kind of decent exit, much less an IPO.

"Erik, look. We've been pretty clear we've been looking for a CTO for a while…"

"What is this place becoming? Unless we go back to dealing with restaurants, I quit."

He stood there stock still, daring her to argue. Demanding she beg him to stay.

She looked back at him, appraising all six-foot-five inches of tobacco-stinking, code-muddling, snake-in-the grass anarchist. And when his shoulders drooped just a little bit, she replied.

"I think you misunderstand my point, Erik. You're fired."

When Hanna and Erik stepped out of the conference room, Jack and Raphael were waiting for them. Raphael had boxed up Erik's things while he was in the meeting, and he handed it to Erik as he walked by.

Erik looked startled. "Hey, can I get some personal stuff off my work laptop?"

Raphael looked at Jack, tilting his head slightly. Jack coughed, as if to clear fear from his throat, and replied, "Sorry. Because of the circumstances of your departure, we cannot allow that."

Erik leaned over Raphael, looming above the slight Hispanic man. "You are fucked, you know."

"Probably." Raphael shrugged. "It is a startup."

Erik threw a last longing glance at the laptop, but he shambled toward the door. Hanna followed him out.

"We'll need to change the security code," Raphael said to Jack.

Jack stood there, letting the reality of it sink it. "Bloody hell. She did it," he said.

"She is the CEO. And Erik was endangering the company. We're too precarious, too new, to let things like that slide."

"I get that. I just think…"

Raphael turned from the door to look him in the eyes.

Jack continued. "I'm going to step down as President. We don't need a President. But we need a Head of Product. What I really care about is making sure we have high quality products." He paused. "But is that what TeaBee needs? I've spent so much time doing stuff we don't need, not paying attention to real problems. I don't know if I can really be CPO. Or VP of Product or whatever it's called."

Raphael sat back on the edge of a desk. "None of us know if we can do it. That's why they say 'fake it until you make it.' You don't think I'd like to go hide in Notepad, just code for a while? Man." He looked down at his shoes for a moment, then back into Jack's eyes. "Just pretend you know what you are doing, and focus on your Objectives. Trust that the OKRs will keep you from sliding back into old habits. That's why I like OKRs so much. They hold me to my promises, even when I feel like sliding back into my comfort zone. Dude, we're all making it up."

Jack let out a long sigh. It felt good to know he wasn't the only one who felt like an impostor.

Raphael picked up a stapler off the desk, and turned it as he continued, "We need to commit to each other, and to our company and our goals. Then, we just execute like madmen."

And with a laugh, he stapled several times into the air.

Jack laughed, too.

Hanna walked back in.

"Well?" asked Jack.

"He's gone. Let's get going. I'm in a mood to get things done."

They headed into the conference room where the rest of the team waited.

Jack opened the meeting by introducing Raphael.

"Hi folks. If you missed the email last night, this is Raphael. He's coming on as interim CTO, and if we behave, perhaps he'll even consider joining permanently." There were a couple polite smiles from Naoko and Cameron, but many of the team had their heads down in their laptops. It was like talking to robots.

Hanna stood. "Folks, we're going to make more changes than just having Rachael join us. First, I'd like everyone to close their laptops. We need everyone's attention." She waited.

All laptops closed, except Sheryl's. "I'm just finishing up a bug…" Sheryl said, holding up a finger.

"I think that bug will be there when the meeting is done."

The room sat silently until Sheryl shut her laptop.

Hanna opened up discussion on the OKRs from last quarter.

"Most folks did not hit their OKRs last quarter…"

The team exploded into excuses.

"We had some problems with the performance of the site!" said Sheryl.

"We had to deal with wrong orders and late deliveries to Los Gatos!" Cameron chimed in.

"I don't think we're marketing right," Anya suggested.

"We didn't hire a second salesperson," added Naoko.

"And that's ok," Hanna interjected.

The team quieted.

"I mean, not ok, but rather… to be expected. I've been asking around." She nodded toward Raphael, "And it seems many teams fail the first time they try to do OKRs. It may take us another quarter to get our OKRs right."

Sheryl said, "Do we have time for this? We're too little for this kinda big company thing, aren't we?"

Hanna was ready for this. "Google started with OKRs when they were a year old, and it worked for them. Many small companies become big companies because of OKRs. And guys, we may not have made our OKRs, but we should be grateful they showed us we've got a problem with focus."

Silence. Hanna continued. "So we're making a few changes to how we do it this quarter. First of all, we are only going to have one OKR for the company. We need to focus on the one thing that will make or break us, and that is our relationship with the suppliers."

She looked around the room. The team's faces mostly looked blank, but Raphael's twinkling smile encouraged her to continue.

"Secondly, we will set OKRs for each group that ties back to the company goal. Third, we are going to set a confidence level for our Key Results. Each one should be five out of ten level of belief we can hit them. All our goals will be stretch goals. Most importantly, we are going to check in on our OKRs and what we are doing to accomplish them every single week, in this meeting."

The team still looked grim. Some, like Sheryl and Cameron leaned forward in their seats. They were with her.

"We have a new format we'd like to use for our weekly status meeting. We'll be sharing our priorities and our confidence changes. This is not a report card. It's a way to help each other meet our goals and stay on track."

She drew a four-square on the white board.

"From now on, we'll use this as our format. It shouldn't take you more than ten minutes each week to update this model. The first one may take a bit longer of course, but after that it's just edits.

"Here in the upper right we'll list our OKRs. As well, we'll list the confidence level we have that we'll actually hit them. Here are our company's from last quarter, as an example."

She wrote:

Objective: Establish clear value to restaurant suppliers as a quality tea provider,

KR: Reorders at 85% 5/10

KR: 20% of reorders self-serve 5/10

KR: Revenue of 250K 5/10

Then she continued, "Notice all my confidence levels are five? That's because I want them to be really bold, but not impossible. If we can hit two out of three, I'll be pretty proud of us. I'll update the company's confidence each week. Raphael will do Engineering's, Jack will do Product's, including Design, Frank will do Sales' and Naoko Finance."

"I want you guys to feel free to ask why my confidence is going up and down. This is a discussion document."

Jack joined her to the left of the board.

"Here in the upper left, we'll list the top three things we're doing this week to meet the Objective. We will mark them with the priority, P1 for must do, P2 for should do. We won't even list it if it's less than that, and we won't list more than our top four. Focus!"

He wrote:

P1: Close deal with TLM Foods

P1: New Order flow spec'd

P1: 3 solid sales candidates in for interview

P2: Create Customer Service job description

He said, "You may want to occasionally add a P2 if you think the group might want to be aware of some task you are doing, but the goal is not to tell people about every little thing. Just the big stuff, the stuff that they can help with, or at least should be aware of. We know you are working hard. We just want to make sure the right things are getting done."

Then he filled out the lower left.

"Here is where you'll give a list of the most important things that you're planning to work on next. This is just to keep us all on the same page, in case we need to buy servers or get marketing ready. List the big things that are happening in the next four weeks or so."

Finally, Hanna pointed to the right hand bottom. "These are going to be our health metrics. We'll be driving the team forward pretty hard, so we want to make sure everyone is ok, not getting burned out or feeling left out. What do you think our second health metric should be?"

There was a vigorous conversation where people threw out things they thought should be tracked, like code health and customer satisfaction, but finally they committed to the happiness of the restaurant suppliers.

That would keep everyone focused on the new customers.

"We'll set it red, yellow or green. I know that is a bit imprecise, but we want to get a gut feeling about how we are doing and talk about how to fix it. For example, on customer satisfaction, red would be if we are losing customers, yellow if we think we are about to." She paused, feeling a little nervous. She had no idea how the next part of the conversation would go. "Where should we set it today?" asked Hanna

"Yellow," said Cameron. Jack and Hanna turned to their normally easygoing engineer. "Um, well, when you guys are out selling, I answer the phone. Sheryl doesn't like to, and Erik's always got headphones on. Always *had.* And the suppliers, they ask me stuff about how the website works a lot. I don't think they actually like it."

Jack grimaced ruefully. He was supposed to be the one paying attention to users. "I know. We'll fix that this quarter."

"And team health is red?" Jack ventured. "Because of the changes?"

"Yellow," Sheryl retorted. "Erik wasn't as important as he thought he was. We'll see how new guy does." And she smiled, and the team laughed as they realized she was joking.

Hanna finally relaxed. If the taciturn Sheryl was joking, maybe they had a shot at this working. "Ok, folks, now let's set this quarter's OKRs!"

Cameron frowned. "Aren't you going to give them to us? Like last quarter?"

"Nope," Hanna replied. "Let me ask you a dumb question. Should we replace this conference table?"

"Hell no," said Cameron.

"Why not?" asked Hanna. "It's wobbly, and if we hire two more salespeople, we're not going to all fit around it."

"We can't ditch it! I remember when we first moved in the office. It took Jack and me three hours to figure out the instructions and get it built."

"There you go. We value the things we make together. We're going to set our Objectives together. We're going to pick Key Results as a team. And we are going make them as a team, too. This is our company. We succeed or fail together."

And then team went to work on their new OKRs and priorities.

HANNA, FRIDAY, ONE MONTH LATER

"Demo!" Raphael shouted. His engineers got up and started hooking up a laptop to the big screen TV and pulling chairs around it.

"That means everybody!" he hollered. "Come on you, Sales!" He hadn't quite managed to remember everybody's name yet. And then, "Hanna, put down that spreadsheet and join us! Beer!"

Hanna had forgotten about demo day. Raphael had warned he'd be taking over the office Fridays around four. He planned to demo the work the engineers had done that week. She stretched, sighed at the work she now wouldn't be doing, and strolled over to the back of the group. A normal Friday was the founders working late, as various employees sheepishly left one by one. The week ended with a whimper, not a bang. Would today be different?

The engineers shared the code they'd written, demoing snippets from the new restaurant supplier support interface. Even taciturn Sheryl shared a rework of the database to allow for an API for the supplier reorder system. Hanna was relieved. Finally, work toward their actual Objectives!

Then as Hanna thought things were going to end, Jack jumped up. He gestured Anya to plug in. "We've got a few new directions for the restaurant supplier information pages we'd like to share."

Hanna was excited to view the mocks. Yet more progress toward their shared Objectives! As well, she'd been kind of wondering what Jack and Anya did all day. Seeing the design in various stages of completeness made her realize it was pretty complicated stuff. In fact, she felt better about both teams. Which made her wonder what everyone else did all day.

When they were done discussing the new designs, Hanna moved to the front of the group.

"Folks, this was great! But I know we've got more to share. Frank? Any sales?"

"Well, I've gotten a little company called Tasteco to sign."

Hanna barked an uncharacteristically loud laugh. "Damn! I've been after them forever! That gets us into the Midwest! Congrats!"

Then Jack interjected, "Well, Hanna? What have you been up to?"

Hanna shook her head. Only Jack could put her on the spot like that.

"I found us a part-time customer service person! Her name is Carol Lundgren, and she built E-Pen's customer service team. She's a mom who's putting her kid into preschool, so she's looking for a place that is willing to be flexible with her working hours. So we were able to scoop her up!" The team burst into spontaneous applause.

So the TeaBee team went on, drinking beer and sharing the week's stories. Hanna found herself giddy with all the amazing progress they'd made. And more importantly, the mood of the room had changed. It was hard to believe just a month ago they'd been moping around, feeling incompetent.

Jack came up to where Hanna perched on the edge of a desk and sat next to her, close enough to speak quietly and not be overheard.

"I ended Anya's contract early. Today is her last day."

"What? The mocks looked great!"

"Yes, but I can take over if we need any revisions. The work she was doing was not a P1. It wasn't helping the OKRs."

Hanna looked at the leaves floating in the bottom of her cup of Dragon's Fog. She thought perhaps she saw tiny gallows and she frowned.

"Hey now! Don't fret! Designers are the hottest commodity in the Valley! She's already got another gig. If we don't focus on keeping this company afloat, she won't be the only one job hunting."

Hanna smiled softly. "You are singing my tune."

The team made Fridays part of their weekly rhythm. Each Monday, they'd plan together and commit to each other. They had the hard conversations a young company has to. And each Friday, they'd celebrate. Some weeks, when it felt like they were never going to make their OKRs, the Friday "wins session" (as they started to call it) gave everybody the hope to keep trying. It was incredibly motivating. Everyone wanted to have a win to share and would work hard during the week to find one. The team began to feel like they were part of something magical.

HAPPILY EVER AFTER?

A quarter later, the team had a very different check in. They had accomplished every Key Result. The team was jubilant and burst into excited chatter.

Raphael poured water on their excitement. "Hey guys, this isn't good. Are we sandbagging?"

"Sandbagging?" Jack asked.

"You know, setting goals we know we can make. To feel good about ourselves. Instead of setting real stretch goals."

The room fell silent. Hanna gritted her teeth. She silently prepared to overcome in inevitable morale drop.

Then Jack spoke up again. "Well then, we'll just have to set proper brutal goals this time. I've seen you on Fridays. We can kill it!" Hearing their dour brit use Silicon Valley slang made everyone laugh. The team dug in, and set their hardest goals yet.

HANNA, SIX MONTHS LATER

The next quarter, the team gathered again to review their quarterly goals. As Hanna predicted, the team did not fit around the conference table. Carol sat with her customer service team at chairs against the wall, slightly behind the sales team. Mindy, the newest member of Customer Service flirted unapologetically with Frank. But Hanna couldn't bring herself to worry. While this time around they had only hit two of the company's Key Results, they were two critical ones that Hanna had doubted were possible to achieve.

Jack nearly tap danced as he led the team through setting the next quarter's goals. Not only were the suppliers all re-ordering through the site, TeaBee had gotten their first new business lead through it.

Meanwhile, Raphael had flown down to Argentina and made connections with local farmers there. Now they had small producers of Yerba Mate providing their herbal tea for the suppliers to buy. Sarah, their new head of marketing, had a game plan to create a Yerba Mate craze.

It wasn't all celebrations. Sheryl had gotten bored, now that the hard problems were done, and she resigned. But she left on decent terms, and between the Friday celebrations and Raphael's tireless reminders of the company Objectives, the engineering team grew and thrived. TeaBee was a good place to work and was becoming a good place for the tea growers of the world.

HANNA, ONE YEAR LATER

Hanna sat at her desk, staring at her email. It was done. They had closed the Series A. They were funded! They were set for at least a year! She spun around in her chair to look for her boys. Jack and Raphael sat hunched over a monitor, and Raphael was pointing at something on the screen. "No smudging!" Jack scolded, and they both laughed.

Hanna sighed. Everything was easier now. Each week they shared their goals. Each week they pushed each other and supported each other. Each week, the numbers went up. She watched the guys talk back and forth about the new buyer dashboard, easily exchanging ideas. Even disagreements were easier now.

Hanna sat back in her chair and cupped her hands around her freshly brewed Longjing. Perhaps she'd save the good news. Tomorrow was the Friday wins session. It'd be nice to have the best news to brag about.

THE FRAMEWORK FOR RADICAL FOCUS

WHY WE CAN'T GET THINGS DONE

We all have things we want. Maybe it's a trip to Thailand or to go back to school. Yet year after year passes and that goal is still only a goal, and not a reality.

If you are a CEO or a manager, you want things for your company. You want to move into that new market, or figure out mobile, or build a competency in an area you are weak, such as design or customer service. Yet even in the most successful companies, the thing we have determined must happen, often doesn't.

Why is this? If it is important, then why doesn't it happen? I believe there are five reasons.

One: We haven't prioritized our goals.

There is an old saying, "If everything is important, nothing is important." Too often we have many competing goals that all seem equally important. And they may *feel* equally important, but if I asked you to stack rank them instead of choose between them, you could probably put them in order of importance. Once you've prioritized them, choosing to work on them one at a time has a much higher incidence of success.

It's the same with a company, only worse. With so many people running around, you are sure you can get many goals to move forward. But the reality is, running a company takes work all by itself. Each day people are running hard to stay in place: fulfilling orders, stroking customers, minding hardware. Add to that the background noise of a half dozen goals, and you assure very little beyond the bare necessities will happen.

By setting a single Objective with only three Key Results to measure it, you can provide the kind of focus needed to achieve great things despite life's little distractions.

Two: We haven't communicated the goal obsessively and comprehensively.

"When you are tired of saying it, people are starting to hear it" – Jeff Weiner, CEO of LinkedIn

Once you have picked the goal you want your team to focus on, you have to reiterate it daily. But it's not enough to talk about it, you must weave reminders into every aspect of the company life. Progress toward the goal must be marked in status meetings and weekly status emails. Projects must be evaluated against the goal. To set a goal and then ignore it is an easy recipe for failure.

By continually repeating the goal every Monday in the commitment meetings, in the weekly status emails and in the Friday wins celebrations, we assure that the goal is in the front of everyone's mind and tied to all activities.

Three: We don't have a plan to get things done.

Once we know the one thing we must make happen, we think willpower is enough. Just Do It, right? Wrong.

When people want to lose weight, they do better with Weight Watchers than willpower. When people want to get fit, they do better with personal trainers than willpower. That's because willpower is a finite resource. This was shown in a famous 1996 study by Roy Baumeister, in which subjects forbidden to eat a bowl of radishes were able to work twice as long on unsolvable math problems than those who had been forbidden to eat freshly baked chocolate cookies. (I also learned that it doesn't take much willpower to skip eating radishes.) After a long day of not quitting your job, killing your coworkers or hitting Reply All on that email chain, trying to turn down a slice of birthday cake is beyond anyone's will.

You need a process that helps you make sense of the work you need to do, and keeps you on track even when you are tired. The process reminds you what to do, even when you don't feel like doing it. The original OKR system was just a way to set smart stretch goals. But the system around it—commitment, celebrations, check ins—makes sure you continue to make progress toward your goals even when you feel more like eating a cookie.

Four: We haven't made time for what matters.

"What is important is seldom urgent, and what is urgent is seldom important." – Dwight Eisenhower

The Eisenhower Box is a common time management tool. Most people focus on the lower right, where you stop doing what is unimportant and not urgent. But how many people take the upper left seriously and schedule what *must* be done? Urgent things get done, both important and unimportant, because we feel keenly the pressure of time. Unless we bring that pressure to other important things, they will continue living in the land of tomorrow. And because we live in the land of today, we never do them. Block out time to do what matters.

There is nothing as invigorating as a deadline. By committing every Monday to work toward the Objective, you assure you'll be held accountable to progress.

Five: We give up instead of iterate.

"Happy families are all alike; every unhappy family is unhappy in its own way." – Leo Tolstoy

When I work with clients to implement OKRs, I give them a warning: you will fail the first time. They do all fail, but they all fail in their own special way.

Maybe a company will find they have sandbaggers, and they manage to make all their Key Results in the first try, because no one ever sets hard goals. This is a company that is afraid to fail, and has never learned what a stretch goal really is. The next cycle, they have to push themselves farther.

Maybe a company is the opposite, and no one makes their Key Results, because they are constantly over-promising and under-delivering. This is a company lying to itself. It needs to learn what it is actually capable of.

The most common fail is no follow-through. I've seen any number of companies set OKRs, then ignore them the rest of the quarter. When the last week of the quarter shows up, they seem surprised when no progress has been made.

However, the successful ones all have the same characteristic: they try again. The only hope for success is iteration. This does not mean blindly trying the same thing over and over again. I believe that is the definition of insanity. Instead, you track closely what works, and what does not, and you do more of what works and less of what doesn't. The heart of success is learning.

A Path to Success

It's not complicated. It's merely hard. Very hard. You have to pick what goal matters most, and not be greedy and unrealistic and try to do everything. You have to get clear in your mind and your message, then communicate it out over and over until everyone is on the same page. You have to dedicate time to accomplishing the goal, instead of endless hoping for a tomorrow that never comes. You have to have a plan that will keep you moving forward, even when you are tired and disheartened. And you have to be ready for failure, ready to learn and ready to try again.

We start our journey to our dreams by wanting, but we arrive by focusing, planning and learning.

Before Starting OKRs, Check Your Mission

Most startups resist creating a company mission. It seems like an exercise in big company propaganda, and not something Lean and Agile folks should be fiddling around with. But this is a misconception. Almost all startups start with a mission, even if they haven't written it down.

If you think that you create a startup to make money, you are misinformed. Ninety percent of startups fail, according to a recent study by Allmand Law. If it's a payout you want, it's a much safer proposition to join a Wall Street consulting firm. But if you want to change the world—an already ridiculous goal—you can do worse than starting a company to do it. Which means you think the world needs changing. Which means you probably have a mission in your back pocket.

It probably started with the founders saying, "If only students could figure out which teachers are actually good," or "I wish there was an easier way to share videos with my parents in Poland," or "I wish I could get decent tea at my favorite café." Then a little poking around led to the realization there was a market who wanted the same problem solved. Finally, that leads to a mission, "Know who knows how to make you know," or "Connecting far flung families through easily shared memories," or "Bringing great tea to people who love it." They don't have to be great works of poetry. They do have to be simple, memorable and act as guide when you make a decision about how to spend your time.

A good mission is short enough everyone in the company can keep it in their head. Great missions are inspirational, yet directed. Google's is so powerful that even non-Googler's know it: "To organize the world's information and make it universally accessible and useful."

Amazon's is: "To be Earth's most customer-centric company, where customers can find and discover anything they might want to buy online, and endeavors to offer its customers the lowest possible prices," which, even if you forget the rest, you can remember the first part about being customer centric. Zynga's is the simple: "Connecting the world through games." And if you get a coffee at Philz, you can ask anyone there and they'll tell you their mission is to: "better people's day."

Your mission is short and memorable. When you have a question in your daily work life, the mission should be top of mind to help you answer.

To make one, start with this simple formula:

We [reduce pain/improve life] in [market] by [value proposition].

Then refine. As you can see from some of the shorter missions above, just value proposition can be enough.

Now I know you may change markets, or add a business model as you go along, but try to make a mission that can hold you for at least five years. In many ways, a mission and an Objective in the OKR model have a lot in common; they are aspirational and memorable. The key difference is time scale. An Objective takes you through a year or a quarter. A mission should last a lot longer.

A mission keeps you on the rails. The OKRs provide focus and milestones. Using OKRs without a mission is like using jet fuel without a jet. It's messy, undirected and potentially destructive. Once you have a mission, selecting each quarter's Objectives is straightforward.

You are no longer faced with a crazy world of possibilities. You can have a conversation about what will move the mission forward. You can fight about sequencing. But once the dust has settled, you can pick the one big bold thing you will do because you know where you are going.

OKR Fundamentals

The OKR approach to setting goals has been used at Google, Zynga, General Assembly and beyond, and is spreading like wildfire across successful Silicon Valley companies. The companies that have adopted the approach are growing like weeds.

OKR stands for **Objectives** and **Key Results**. The form of the OKR has been more or less standardized. The Objective is qualitative, and the KRs (most often three) are quantitative. They are used to focus a group or individual around a bold goal. The Objective establishes a goal for a set period of time, usually a quarter. The Key Results tell you if the Objective has been met by the end of the time.

Your **Objective** is a single sentence that is:

- **Qualitative and Inspirational**

The Objective is designed to get people jumping out of bed in the morning with excitement. And while CEOs and VCs may jump out of bed in the morning with joy over a 3% gain in conversion, most mere mortals get excited by a sense of meaning and progress. Use the language of your team. If they want to use slang and say "pwn it" or "kill it," use that wording.

- **Time Bound**

For example, doable in a month, a quarter. You want it to be a clear sprint toward a goal. If it takes a year, your Objective may be a strategy or maybe even a mission.

- **Actionable by the Team Independently**

This is less a problem for startups, but bigger companies often struggle because of interdependence. Your Objective has to be truly yours, and you can't have the excuse of "Marketing didn't market it."

An Objective is like a mission statement, only for a shorter period of time. A great Objective inspires the team, is hard (but not impossible) to do in a set time frame, and can be done by the person or people who have set it, independently.

Here are some good Objectives:

- Pwn the direct-to-business coffee retail market in the South Bay.
- Launch an awesome MVP.
- Transform Palo Alto's coupon using habits.
- Close a round that lets us kill it next quarter.

and some poor Objectives:

- Sales numbers up 30%.
- Double users.
- Raise a Series B of 5M.

Why are those bad Objectives bad? Probably because they are actually Key Results.

Key Results

Key Results take all that inspirational language and quantify it. You create them by asking a simple question, "How would we know if we met our Objective?" This causes you to define what you mean by "awesome," "kill it," or "pwn." Typically you have three Key Results. Key Results can be based on anything you can measure, including:

- Growth
- Engagement
- Revenue
- Performance
- Quality

That last one can throw people. It seems hard to measure quality. But with tools like NPS, it can be done. (NPS = Net Promoter Score, a number based on customer's willingness to recommend a given product to friends and family. See HBR's "The Only Number You Need to Grow" Harvard Business Review, December 2003.)

If you select your KRs wisely, you can balance forces like growth and performance, or revenue and quality, by making sure you have the potentially opposing forces represented.

"Launch an Awesome MVP" might have KRs of:

- 40% of users come back 2X in one week
- Recommendation score of 8
- 15% conversion

Notice how hard those are?

KRs Should Be Difficult, Not Impossible

OKRs are always stretch goals. A great way to do this is to set a confidence level of five of ten on the OKR. By confidence level of five out of ten, I mean "I have confidence I only have a 50/50 shot of making this goal." A confidence level of one means "never gonna happen, my friend." A confidence level of ten means "yeah, gonna nail this one." It also means you are setting your goals way too low, which is often called sandbagging. In companies where failure is punished, employees quickly learn not to try. If you want to achieve great things, you have to find a way to make it safe to reach further than anyone has before.

As you set the KR, you are looking for the sweet spot where you are pushing yourself and your team to do bigger things, yet not making it impossible. I think that sweet spot is when you have a 50/50 shot of failing.

Take a look at your KRs. If you are getting a funny little feeling in the pit of your stomach saying, "We are really going to have to all bring our A game to hit these…" then you are probably setting them correctly. If you look at them and think "we're doomed," you've set them too hard. If you look them and think, "I can do that with some hard work," they are too easy.

What Makes OKRs Work?

OKRs Cascade.

The company should set an OKR, and then each department should determine how *their* OKR leads to the company's successful OKR. A team can focus their

OKR on a single Key Result or try to support the entire set. For example, Engineering might decide satisfaction is tightly connected with speed (and they'd be right.) So set an OKR like:

Performance Upon Launch Equivalent to an Established Company

- 99.8% uptime
- <1 second response time
- Instantaneous perceived load time (measure by survey, 90% users say page loaded "immediately")

(I'm not an engineer so please do not mock my KRs too hard.)

As you can imagine, some teams, like Product Management, can easily align their OKRs with the company OKRs, while others may have to dig a little deeply to make sure they are supporting the company goal. Much of the value in OKRs comes from the conversations on what matters, how it will be measured and what it means for the teams who are used to working from their own standards, apart from the business goals. Customer Service, Design and Engineering often have to work a little harder to find meaningful OKRs that will move the business goal forward. But it's worth doing. Can Customer Service upsell disgruntled customers to a better plan? Can Design create an onboarding flow that improves retention? Can Engineering increase satisfaction with a better recommendations algorithm? No department can be an island.

As well, each individual should set individual OKRs that reflect both personal growth and support the company's goals. If the company's OKRs are around acquisition, a product manager might decide she wants to "Get great at sales." She then might choose KRs of completing sales training with a high score, as well as improving the conversion rate of the product she runs.

Individual OKRs are about becoming better at your job, as well as helping your product get better. It's also a gift to managers struggling with a difficult employee. In the individual OKR- setting process, she can work with that person to set goals that correct those problems *before* they blossom into full disciplinary actions. By setting measurable KRs, she can avoid accusations of personal bias if things do not improve.

OKRs Are Part of Your Regular Rhythm

When people fail to achieve their Objectives, it's often because they set OKRs at the beginning of the quarter, and then forget about them. In those three months, you are barraged by teammate requests, the CEO sends you articles you should read and incorporate, you get customer complaints… there are always 101 interesting things to spend your time on that do not lead to success. I highly recommend baking your OKRs into your weekly team meetings (if you have them) and your weekly status emails. Adjust your confidence levels every single week. Have discussions about why they are going up or down.

OKRs Provide an Unmoving and Clear Goal

Do not change OKRs halfway through the quarter. If you see you've set them badly, suck it up and either fail or nail them, and use that learning to set them better next time. No team gets OKRs perfect the first time. Changing them dilutes focus, and keeping teams focused is the entire point of the OKR. Changing them halfway through teaches your team not to take the OKRs seriously.

Get Ready to Fail… BIG!

Let's be honest: we hate to fail. Everyone in the Silicon Valley gives lip service to failure, but really we still don't enjoy it. OKRs aren't about hitting targets, but about learning what you are really capable of. Failure is a positive indicator of stretching. OKRs are designed to push you to do more than you knew you were capable of. If you shoot for the moon, you may not make it but it's a hell of a view.

OKRS FOR PRODUCT TEAMS

By Marty Cagan, Founder of the Silicon Valley Product Group

During the course of the past 30 years, Marty Cagan has served as an executive responsible for defining and building products for some of the most successful companies in the world, including Hewlett-Packard, Netscape Communications, America Online, and eBay.

OKRs are a very general tool that can be used by anyone in the organization, in any role, or even for your use in your personal life. However, as with any tool, there are considerations as to the best ways to apply. OKRs have enjoyed considerable success especially inside technology product organizations, from large to small, and there have been some important lessons learned as teams and organizations work to improve their ability to execute.

The central organizational concept in a product organization is a *product team*(aka durable product team, dedicated product team, agile product team, or squad). A product team is a *cross-functional* set of professionals, typically comprised of a product manager, a product designer, and a small number of engineers. Sometimes there are additional people with specialized skills included on the team, such as a data scientist, a user researcher or a test automation engineer. Each product team typically is responsible for some significant part of the company's product offering or technology. For example, one product team might be responsible for the mobile apps, another might be responsible for security technology, and another might be responsible for search technology, and so on.

The key is that these people with their different skill sets usually come from different functional departments in the company, but they sit and work all day, every day, with their cross-functional team to solve hard business and technology problems. It's not unusual in larger organizations to have on the order of 20 to 50 of these cross-functional product teams, each responsible for different areas, and each product team with its own objectives. The problems these teams are asked to tackle are, as you might expect, communicated and tracked through the product team's OKRs. The OKRs also help to ensure that each team is aligned with the objectives of the company. Moreover, as an organization scales, the OKRs become an increasingly necessary tool to ensure that each product team understands how they are contributing to the greater whole, for coordinating work across teams, and in avoiding duplicate work.

The reason this is all important to explain is that when organizations first start with OKRs, there's a common tendency to have each *functional department* create their own OKRs for their own organization. For example, the design department might have Objectives related to moving to a responsive design; the engineering department might have Objectives related to improving the scalability and performance of the architecture; and the quality department might have Objectives relating to the test and release automation.

The problem is that the *individual members* of each of these functional departments are the actual members of a cross-functional product team. The product team has business related Objectives (for example, to reduce the customer acquisition cost, or to increase the number of daily active users, or to reduce the time to onboard a new customer), but each person on the team may have their own set of Objectives that are cascading down through their functional manager.

Imagine if the engineers were told to spend their time on re-platforming, and the designers on moving to a responsive design, and QA on re-tooling, and so on. While each of these may be worthy activities, the chances of actually solving the business problems that the cross-functional teams were created to solve are not high. What all too often happens in this case is that the actual people on the product teams are conflicted as to where they should be spending their time, resulting in confusion, frustration and disappointing results from leadership and individual contributors alike.

But this is easily avoided.

If you are deploying OKRs for your product organization, the key is to focus your OKRs at the *product team* level. Focus the attention of the individuals on their product team Objectives. If different functional organizations (like design, engineering or quality assurance) have larger Objectives (like responsive design, technical debt, and test automation) they should be discussed and prioritized at the leadership team level along with the other business Objectives, and incorporated into the relevant *product team's* Objectives.

Note that it's not a problem for *managers* of the functional areas to have individual Objectives relating to their organization, because these people aren't conflicted, as they're not normally serving on a product team. For example, the head of UX design might be responsible for a strategy for migrating to a responsive design; the head of engineering might be responsible for delivering a strategy around managing technical debt; the head of Product Management might be responsible for delivering a product vision; or the head of QA might be responsible for selecting a test automation tool.

It's also not normally a big problem if individual contributors (such as a particular engineer or designer or product manager) were to have a small number of personal growth related Objectives (such as improving their knowledge of a particular technology), just as long as the individual isn't committing to a burden that will interfere with their ability to contribute their part to their product team, which of course is their primary responsibility.

The key is that the cascading of OKRs in a product organization needs to be up from the cross-functional product teams to the company or business unit level.

SETTING A RHYTHM OF EXECUTION

Many companies who try OKRs fail, and they blame the system. But no system works if you don't actually keep to it. Setting a goal at the beginning of a quarter and expecting it to magically be achieved by the end is naïve. As I covered in the story of Hanna and Jack's company, it's important to have a cadence of commitment and celebration.

Scrum is a technique used by engineers to commit to progress and hold each other both accountable and to support each other. Each week an engineer shares what happened last week, what they commit to doing next week, and any blockers that keep them from their goals. In larger orgs, they hold a "scrum of scrums" to assure teams are also holding each other accountable for meeting goals. There is no reason multidisciplinary groups can't do the same.

Monday Commitments

Each Monday, the team should meet to check in on progress against OKRs, and commit to the tasks that will help the company meet its Objective. I recommend a format with four key quadrants:

Intention for the week: What are the 3-4 most important things you must get done this week toward the Objective? Discuss if these priorities will get you closer to the OKRs.

Forecast for month: What should your team know is coming up that they can help with or prepare for?

Status toward OKRs: If you set a confidence of five out of ten, has that moved up or down? Have a discussion about why.

Health metrics: Pick two things you want to protect as you strive toward greatness. What can you not afford to eff-up? Key relationships with customers? Code stability? Team well-being? Now mark when things start to go sideways, and discuss it

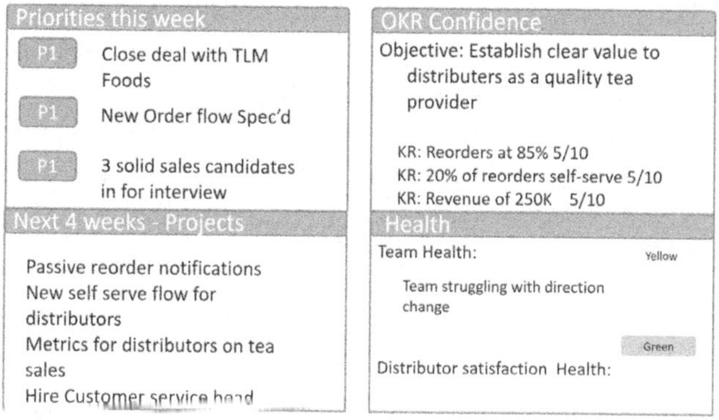

This document is first and last a conversation tool. You want to talk about issues like:

Do the priorities lead to our hitting our OKRs?

Why is confidence dropping in our ability to make our OKRs? Can anyone help?

Are we prepared for major new efforts? Does Marketing know what Product is up to?

Are we burning out our people, or letting hacks become part of the code bases?

When you meet, you could discuss only the four-square, or you can use it to provide a status overview, then supplement with other detailed documents covering metrics, a pipeline of projects or related updates. Each company has a higher or lower tolerance for status meetings.

Try to keep things as simple as possible. Too many status meetings are about team members trying to justify their existence by listing every little thing they've done. Trust your team makes good choices in their everyday lives. Set the tone of the meeting to be about team members helping each other to meet the shared goals they all have committed to.

Have fewer priorities and shorter updates.

Make time for the conversations. If only a fourth of the time allotted for the Monday meeting is presentations and the rest is discussing next steps, you are doing it right. If you end early, it's a good sign. Just because you've set aside an hour doesn't mean you have to use it.

Fridays Are for Winners

When teams are aiming high, they fail a lot. While this it's good to aim high, missing your goals without also seeing how far you've come is often depressing. That's why committing to the Friday wins session is so critical.

In the Friday wins session, teams all demo whatever they can. Engineers show bits of code they've got working and designers show mockups and maps. But beyond that, every team should share something. Sales can talk about who they've closed, Customer Service can talk about customers they've rescued, Business Development shares deals. This have several benefits. One, you start to feel like you are part of a pretty special winning team. Two, the team starts looking forward to having something to share. They seek wins. And lastly, the company starts to appreciate what each discipline is going through and understands what everyone does all day.

Providing beer, wine, cake, or whatever is appropriate to your team on a Friday is also important to making the team feel cared for. If the team is really small and can't afford anything, you can have a "Friday Wins Jar" that all contribute to. But as the team gets bigger the company should pay for the celebration nibbles as a signal of support. Consider this: the humans who work on the project are the biggest asset. Shouldn't you invest in them?

OKRs are great for setting goals, but without a system to achieve them, they are as likely to fail as any other process that is in fashion. Commit to your team, commit to each other and commit to your shared future. And renew those vows every week.

HOW TO HOLD A MEETING TO SET OKRS FOR THE QUARTER

Setting OKRs is hard. It involves taking a close look at your company, and it involves having difficult conversations about the choices that shape the direction the company should go. Be sure to structure the meeting thoughtfully to get the best results. You will be living these OKRs for the next quarter.

Keep the meeting small – ten or fewer people if possible. It should be run by the CEO, and must include the senior executive team. Take away phones and computers. It will encourage people to move quickly and pay attention.

A few days before the meeting, solicit all the employees to submit the Objective they think the company should focus on. Be sure to give them a very small window to do it in; 24 hours is plenty. You don't want to slow down your process and, in a busy company, later means never.

Have someone (a consultant, the department heads) collect and bring forward the best and most popular ones.

Set aside 4.5 hours to meet. Two 2-hour sessions, with a 30-minute break.

Your goal: cancel the second session. Be focused.

Each exec head should have an Objective or two in mind to bring to the meeting. Have the best employee-generated Objectives written out on Post-it notes, and have your execs add theirs. I recommend having a variety of sizes available, and use the large ones for the Objectives. Cramped writing is hard to read.

Now have the team place the Post-its up on the wall. Combine duplicates, and look for patterns that suggest people are worried about a particular goal. Combine similar Objectives. Stack rank them. Finally, narrow them down to three.

Discuss. Debate. Fight. Stack rank. Pick.

Depending on the team you have, you have either hit the break, or you have another hour left.

Next, have all the members of the exec team freelist as many metrics as they can think of to measure the Objective. Freelisting is a Design Thinking technique. It means to simply write down as many ideas on a topic as you can, one idea per Post-it. You put one idea on each Post-it so you can rearrange, discard, and otherwise manipulate the data you have generated.

It is a far more effective way to brainstorm, and results in better and more diverse ideas. Give the team slightly more time than is comfortable, perhaps ten minutes. You want to get as many interesting ideas as possible.

Next, you will Affinity map them. This is another Design Thinking technique. All it means is you group Post-its with like Post-its. If two people both write DAU (Daily Active Users), you can put those on top of each other. It's two votes for that metric. DAU, MAU, WAU are all engagement metrics, and you can put them next to each other. Finally, you can pick your three types of metrics.

Write the KRs as an X first, i.e. "X revenue" or "X acquisitions" or "X DAU." It's easier to first discuss what to measure, then what the value should be and if it's really a "shoot for the moon" goal. One fight at a time.

As a rule of thumb, I recommend having a usage metric, a revenue metric and a satisfaction metric for the KRs; but obviously that won't always be the right choice for your Objective. The goal is to find different ways to measure success, in order to have sustained success across quarters. For example, two revenue metrics means you might have an unbalanced approach to success. Focusing only on revenue can lead to employees gaming the system and developing short term approaches that can damage retention.

Next, set the values for the KRs. Make sure they really are "shoot for the moon" goals. You should have only 50% confidence you can make them. Challenge each other. Is someone sandbagging? Is someone playing it safe? Is someone foolhardy? Now is the time for debate, not halfway through the quarter.

Finally, take five minutes to discuss the final OKR set. Is the Objective aspirational and inspirational? Do the KRs make sense? Are they hard? Can you live with this for a full quarter?

Tweak until they feel right. Then go live them.

You'll find a worksheet to help you out at:
http://eleganthack.com/an-okr-worksheet

CONNECTING COMPANY BUSINESS OBJECTIVES WITH SERVICE DEPARTMENT OKRS

Teams like Design, Engineering, Finance and Customer Service sometimes struggle to understand how they can contribute to the business goals. By asking hard questions about how a group contributes, and encouraging them to be creative, you can get better and richer buy-in by support groups. Here, Ben Lamorte, an OKR coach, takes us through a conversation he had with a head of Engineering.

OKR Coaching Example: Quantifying Engineering's Contribution to Sales

By Ben Lamorte, Principal at OKRs.com

Ben Lamorte coaches business leaders to define and make measurable progress on their most important goals. He's coached hundreds of managers at dozens of organizations. For more about Ben, see www.OKRs.com.

Let's look at an excerpt from a real OKRs coaching session to illustrate how coaching leaders, through creating their own OKRs—rather than a CEO dictating their OKRs—can dramatically improve the quality and effectiveness of OKRs. Here's an excerpt from a coaching session for the engineering team at a large software company.

Engineering VP: My key objective is to help our sales team achieve their targets.

OKRs Coach: At the end of the quarter, how would we know if Engineering helped Sales achieve their targets?

Engineering VP: Hmm, that's a good question. (Pause)

OKRs Coach: OK, can you name a particular customer who purchased within the last year where Engineering clearly contributed to the sales process?

Engineering VP: Actually, no. But that would be very good data to have. It's not so much that we help Sales close deals, it's more like we keep the prospect in the mix.

The Engineering VP went on to propose the following Key Results:

"Provide sales support for 5 major prospects in Q2"

"Develop training for sales team by end of Q2"

While these two statements are directional, they are not measurable. Let's look at how the OKRs coach helped the VP translate these two statements into measurable KRs.

Statement 1: "Provide sales support for 5 major prospects in Q2"

OKRs Coach: Is there a distinction between a major prospect and a minor prospect? (Makes this *clear* by addressing ambiguity.)

Engineering VP: Not really.

OKRs Coach: Do you and the VP Sales agree on the definition of a "major prospect?" (Ensures *alignment* across departments is jointly defined.)

Engineering VP: Let's replace "major prospect" with "prospect with $100k+ year 1 revenue potential." Then we can run this definition by the VP Sales.

OKRs Coach: Have you measured the number of these sales support events in the past? (To confirm metric history so we know the KR is *measurable.*)

Engineering VP: No.

OKRs Coach: What is the intended outcome of Engineering providing sales support? (Probes intended outcome of achieving the goal to focus on *results not tasks.*)

Engineering VP: It results in either a continuing sales process or kills the deal.

OKRs Coach: What if all five sales support calls result in dead deals? Will we have achieved this goal? (Boundary condition question to ensure *alignment.*)

Engineering VP: No. The meeting is really not considered a success when we lose the deal for technical reasons. Maybe we should define this as, "provide sales support with no more than three $100k+ prospects deciding to not evaluate our product for technical reasons."

OKRs Coach: While this is heading in the right direction, the Key Result is now framed negatively. I recommend the following positively framed version of this goal: Obtain a baseline on "technical pass rate." For example, if we have meetings with ten $100k+ prospects and eight of them advance without technical objection, the technical pass rate is 80%. (Ensures KR is *positive.*)

The Engineering VP liked the idea of tracking technical pass rate. As a result of this OKRs coaching session, the Engineering VP agreed to confirm with VP Sales that technical pass rate is a useful metric to quantify the extent to which Engineering contributes to sales.

THE TIMING OF OKRS

If you are ready to put into place OKRs, you'll want to plan out the timing for implementation. Assuming you've done a training (or done your research), and everyone understands and *is on board for OKRs*, this is my recommended approach:

1. All employees submit the Objective they think the company should pursue next quarter. This increases buy-in for the OKRs and provides interesting insight into the health of the company culture.

If the company is big, this can go to their boss, and roll up, or can be in a survey, or be collected and correlated by consultant and given to the exec team.

2. Exec team, in a half-day session, discusses the Objectives proposed. They choose one. This requires debate and compromise and deserves plenty of time. Then the team sets the KRs, as outlined previously.

I have seen teams set OKRs in as little as a 90-minute meeting. Things that make OKR setting slow include putting off the meeting, skipping the homework and refusing to make decisions. These are HR issues and should be addressed by management. Your company goal is your company's life. Commit.

3. Executives' homework: introduce the OKR for quarter to their direct reports, and have them develop department OKRs. This also should be done in a 2-hour meeting with the department head and her team, run in essentially the same way: freelisting, grouping, stack ranking, selecting.

4. CEO approval. About one hour, plus follow-up discussions if any department heads are way off base. Set aside an entire day for focusing on just this.

5. Department head gives the company and department OKRs to any subteams, and these teams develop their own.

6. Optional: If company is doing individual OKRs, set them now. Individual OKRs are approved by the manager.

This is a great coaching moment! Go over the OKR in a 1:1. Do *not* just do it by email.

7. All hands meeting in which CEO discusses why the OKR is what it is for that quarter, and calls out a few exemplary ones set by directs. As well, covers last quarters OKRs, and points out a few key wins from the quarter. Keeps tone positive and determined.

This is the standard rhythm you will keep from quarter to quarter going forward. If you cannot set OKRs in less than two weeks, you will want to examine your priorities. Nothing is more critical than setting a goal for the company to rally behind.

Preparing for the next quarter

If you have been running a regular commitment and celebration cadence then you should be able to determine if you have made or wiffed your OKRs two weeks before the end of the quarter. Don't lie to yourself that you might pull a rabbit out of a hat in those last two weeks. Only the occasional miracle can help you hit a truly hard goal in such a short time. No reason to put off the inevitable.

Admit you have missed a KR, or admit you set a KR too low and hit it too easily. Get that learning, and roll it into your next goal-setting exercise.

OKRs are about continuous improvement and learning cycles. They are not about making check marks in a list. So you didn't hit any of your KRs. Ask yourself why, and fix it. So you hit them all? Set harder goals, and move on. Focus on learning, getting smarter and having better things to celebrate every Friday.

The First Time

The first time you try OKRs, you are likely to fail. This is a dangerous situation, as your team may become disillusioned with the approach, and be unwilling to try them again. You don't want to lose a powerful tool just because it takes a little time to master. There are three approaches you can use to reduce this risk.

1. Start with only one OKR for the company. By setting a simple goal for the company, your team sees the executive team holding themselves to a high standard. It won't be surprising when next quarter they

are asked to do the same. And by not cascading it, you both simplify implementation *and* see who chooses to adopt OKRs and who will need coaching.

2. Have *one* team adopt OKRs before the entire company does. Choose an independent team that has all the skills to achieve their goals. You can then trumpet their success if it happens, or wait a cycle or two until they perfect their approach and then roll out OKRs across the company.

3. Start out by applying OKRs to projects, in order to train people on the Objective-Result approach. GatherContent is a great example. Every time they have a major project, they first ask what is the Objective for this project, and how will we know if we've succeeded (see the following essay to learn more).

By starting small and focusing on learning how OKRs will work in your organization, you increase your chances of your company adopting a Results-based approach, and reduce the danger of a disillusioned team.

OKRS FOR MVPS

By Angus Edwardson, Product Director at GatherContent.

We use OKRs in a few different ways at GatherContent and have done various experiments with them over the past few years.

We've used OKRs as a company-wide tool to align everyone's focus, we've had them for each department to allow autonomy, and we've also used them on an employee level, to encourage personal development.

The most consistently effective application of OKRs, however, is using them for the product team's projects. At GatherContent, it's a requirement for anyone initiating a new feature to outline a clear Objective and a set of Key Results to better understand why we are doing this work, and how we hope it will succeed.

At the Centre Of the Product Lifecycle

At GatherContent, we try to reduce the complexity of new features until we have a minimum viable product (MVP) we think is worth launching. Our product team works using Kanban, an Agile Development approach for scheduling. With Kanban, all potential projects are put on a wall and then "picked up" as developers move them from "to Do" to "Doing" to "Done."

When my team is ready to start a new project, we pull that MVP off the roadmap and put it into development.

All the MVPs on the roadmap are displayed on Kanban cards which have required fields, including the standardised description, requirements, and any additional notes and sketches.

This structure makes it easy to communicate to the rest of the business what's coming next, and ensures work can be smoothly passed into development. We also include the Objective for the project and the Key Results we hope to see if it succeeds.

Including OKRs on the Kanban cards forces the team to answer two important questions before anything is built:

1. What are we trying to achieve with this feature?
2. How do we measure success or failure?

Here's how our cards are structured:

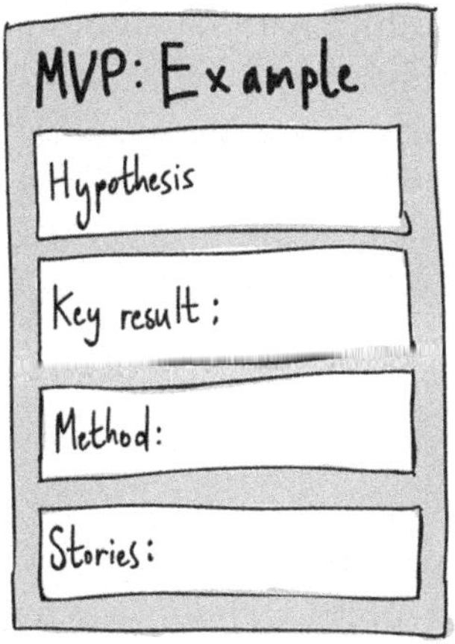

You'll notice that we switched from using "Objective" to using the, ever-so-slightly-semantically-different "Hypothesis." This is to encourage more of an experimental approach to product development. Instead of saying, this will happen, we say, "We think this will happen." Then our hypothesis is proved or disproved. It makes us feel like scientists.

Logic Upfront

As well as the value we get upfront from having all features scoped out with clearly communicated rationale, using OKRs in this context also brings a massive amount of value to other parts of our process.

Prioritizing Work:

An obvious use of these OKRs is that they allow us to prioritize work on the roadmap based on its expected impact. Meaning we can prioritize work based on the goals of the business.

Connecting Product And Business Objectives:

If the business has an Objective to increase the activation rate of new customers, we can prioritize features that we think will have the biggest impact on that area. It's a lovely example of mapping business and departmental OKRs and keeping everyone pleasantly aligned.

Collaborating With 'Others':

People love to talk about what's coming next. While discussions around the roadmap with different people in the business is great, without structure it is prone to stalemating because everyone has a bias toward the areas of the business they are closest to. Being able to quickly recite the business logic behind a feature and its position in the queue can make these conversations much more efficient (and less emotional!).

If someone has something they think is more valuable, you can simply discuss why they think it's valuable (hypothesis) and how valuable it might really be (Key Results). This encourages constructive collaboration.

Measurement and Learning:

The greatest impact of measuring quantifiable targets is in helping us evaluate results, and more importantly, learn from those results.

We track the Key Results of all of our released MVPs in a simple spreadsheet and review it regularly to see what we can learn. We've struggled in the past with the question of when we should measure the results, so we've started setting deadlines for each OKR measurement.

Once the deadline hits and we gather the results, we all get together to discuss any inconsistencies, unexpected outcomes, or other learnings.

Adding OKRs to our Kanban cards has allowed us to prioritize better, learn faster and communicate more effectively. It's also a great way to develop the habit of communicating why we are doing what we are doing.

IMPROVE WEEKLY STATUS EMAILS WITH OKRS

I remember the first time I had to write a status email. I had just been promoted to manager at Yahoo back in 2000 and was running a small team. I was told to "write a status email covering what your team has done that week, due Friday." Well, you can easily imagine how I felt. I had to prove my team was getting things done! Not only to justify our existence, but to prove we needed more people. Because, you know, more people, amiright?

So I did what everyone does: I listed every single thing my reports did, and made a truly unreadable report. Then I started managing managers, and had them send me the same, which I collated into an even longer more horrible report. This I sent to my Design Manager, Irene Au, and my GM, Jeff Weiner (who sensibly requested I put a summary at the top).

And so it went, as I moved from job to job, writing long tedious reports that, at best, got skimmed. At one job, I stopped authoring them. I had my managers send them to my Project Manager, who collated them, sent it to me for review, and after checking for anything embarrassing, I forwarded it on to my boss. One week I forgot to read it, and didn't hear anything about it. It was a waste of everybody's time.

Then I got to Zynga in 2010. Now, say what you want about Zynga, but they were really good at some critical things that make an organization run well. One was the status report. All reports were sent to the entire management team, and I enjoyed reading them. Yes, you heard me right: *I enjoyed reading them*, even if when were 20 of them. Why? Because they had important information laid out in a digestible format. I used them to understand what I needed to do, and learn from what was going right. Please note that Zynga, in the early days, grew faster than any company I've seen. I suspect the efficiency of communication was a big part of that.

When I left Zynga, I started to consult. I adapted the status mail to suit the various companies I worked with, throwing in some tricks from Agile. Now I have a simple, solid format that works across any org, big or small.

1. **Lead with your team's OKRs, and how much confidence you have that you are going to hit them this quarter.**

You list OKRs to remind everyone (and sometimes yourself) *why* you are doing the things you do.

Your confidence is your guess of how likely you feel you will meet your Key Results, on a scale from 1 to 10. A 1 is never going to happen and 10 is in the bag. Mark your confidence red when it falls below 3, green as it passes 7. Color makes it scannable, making your boss and teammates happy. Listing confidence helps you and your teammates track progress and correct early if needed.

2. **List last week's prioritized tasks and if they were achieved.** If they were not, a few words to explain why. The goal here is to learn what keeps the organization from accomplishing what it needs to accomplish. See below for format.

3. **Next list next week's priorities.** Only list three P1s, and make them meaty accomplishments that encompass multiple steps. "Finalize spec for project xeno" is a good P1. It probably encompasses writing, reviews with multiple groups and sign off. It also gives a heads up to other teams and your boss that you'll be coming by.

"Talk to legal" is a bad P1. This priority takes about half hour, has no clear outcome, feels like a subtask and, not only that, you didn't even tell us what you were talking about!

You can add a couple P2s, but they should also be meaty, worthy of being next week's P2s. You want fewer, bigger items.

4. **List any risks or blockers.** Just as in an Agile stand-up, note anything you could use help on that you can't solve yourself. Do *not* play the blame game. Your manager does not want to play mom, listening to you and a fellow executive say "it's his fault."

As well, list anything you know of that could keep you from accomplishing what you set out to do—a business partner playing hard-to-schedule or a tricky bit of technology that might take longer than planned to sort out. Bosses do not like to be surprised. Don't surprise them.

5. **Notes.** Finally, if you have anything that doesn't fit in these categories, but that you absolutely want to include, add a note. "Hired that fantastic guy from Amazon that Jim sent over. Thanks, Jim!" is a decent note, as is, "Reminder: team out Friday for offsite to Giant's game." Make them short, timely and useful. Do

not use notes for excuses, therapy or novel writing practice.

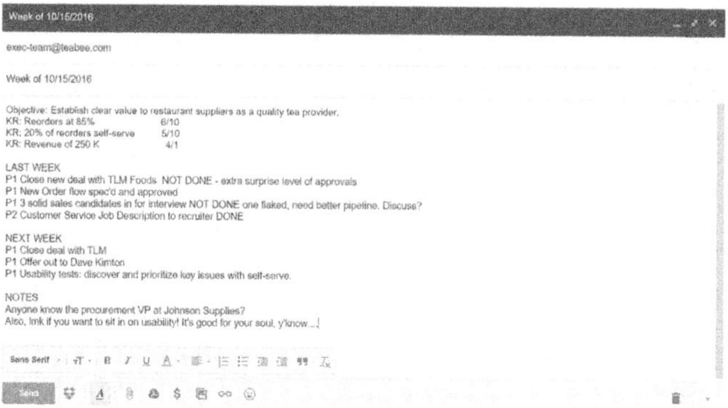

This format also fixes another key challenge large organizations face: coordination. To write a status report the old way, I had to have team status in by Thursday night in order to collate, fact check and edit. But with this system, I know what my priorities are, and I use my reports' statuses only as a way to making sure their priorities are mine. I send out my report Friday, as I receive my reports'. We stay committed to each other, honest and focused.

Work should not be a chore list, but a collective push forward toward shared goals. The status email reminds everyone of this fact and helps us avoid slipping into checkbox thinking.

Coordinating organizational efforts is critical to a company's ability to compete and innovate. Giving up on the status email is a strategic error. It can be a task that wastes key resources, or it can be a way that teams connect and support each other.

COMMON OKR MISTAKES

As I help teams implement OKRs, I've had a huge number of great conversations about the challenges they've faced. There are common mistakes that lead to failure. I define failure as making none of the OKRs or all of the OKRs, or the OKR process having no useful impact on the business.

- **You set too many goals per quarter**

Try setting only one. You want the OKRs to be so clear, everyone in the company carries it around in their head. If you've got five, that isn't going to happen.

Google may need multiple OKRs for the company because they are running a search engine *and* a supporting browser *and* trying to crack social *and* making self-driving cars. Imagine if they set a single Objective of "Make all products supremely social." The self-driving cars folks might create Kitt, a car with personality that will be your friend. A social car might be nifty, but it's probably not something that the market wants. So if you have very different businesses for very different markets, you will need a different OKR set per market/business.

That said, most companies (and all startups) benefit from a single bold OKR to unify and direct effort.

- **You set OKRs for a week or a month**

I'm not totally convinced that a startup should use OKRs before achieving product/market fit, unless that Objective is "find product/market fit." If you can't keep on track longer than a week, you probably aren't ready for OKRs. If you do have product/market fit, then commit to the full three months. After all, what truly bold thing can you do in less than that? If it can be done in a week, it's probably just a task.

- **You set a metric-driven Objective**

This is the downfall of many an MBA. You love numbers. You love money. Doesn't everyone? The OKR unifies multidisciplinary teams, and that means the dreamy designers, the idealist engineers and the caring customer service. The Objective needs to be inspirational, a call-to-action that gets folks to leap out of bed, ready for a new day and a new challenge.

- **You don't set confidence levels**

I've heard plenty of stories of companies where people are expected to hit 70% of their Key Results, so they sandbag two and make one impossibly hard. Not the point, folks. OKRs are there to encourage you to shoot for the moon. So you can learn what you are really capable of.

Setting a confidence level of five out of ten means you have a 50% chance of hitting the goal. That's stretching yourself.

- **You don't track changing confidence levels**

Nothing sucks more than coming into the last month of the quarter and suddenly realizing you forgot to pay attention to the OKRs. Mark changes as you get new information. Remind teammates they've been at five for a long time. Offer help.

- **You use the four-square on Monday as a status report, not as a conversation**

Discuss what needs discussing. Are the priorities really going to move the Key Results? Is the roadmap of upcoming projects going to require coordination? How is the team's health, and why?

- **You talk tough on Friday**

We're tough on ourselves and each other all week. Let's crack a beer and toast what we *did* accomplish. Especially if we aren't going to hit all our Key Results, let's be proud of what setting big goals did let us accomplish.

OKRS AND THE ANNUAL REVIEW

By Deidre Paknad, CEO of Workboard

Workboard enables and sustains OKRs, brings goals into people's day-to-day work focus, and provides continuous and cross-organization transparency.

Somewhere over the past decade, business goals were hijacked and lost their magic powers. In our personal lives they are aspirations, drivers of important decisions and provide purpose. Yet at work and especially in large enterprises, two-thirds of people think they've become largely irrelevant to all but the compensation process. One of the most potent motivators and sources of satisfaction has been neutered in many large organizations – removed from the tool set that individuals and leaders have to grow themselves, their teams and their business.

When performance assessments drive goals instead of goals driving business performance, goals are created for annual reviews. When they're written to ensure compensation outcomes 12 months in the future, goals are necessarily vague and the achievement bar is low. As the velocity of business increases, annual goals get more disconnected from business reality and more watered-down. While this is particularly true in large businesses, it should be said that in many younger organizations, goals are something the CEO shares with the board instead of the team. Either way, they don't help people make good day-to-day decisions about their time and effort or build up to great outcomes.

How do we Restore the Magic Power of Goals?

It starts with reframing goals from a device to assess performance to one that inspires and amplifies it. That means transforming the model, cadence and presence of goals within your organization. Combine aspirational near-term goals with aggressive quantitative metrics and a weekly execution and accountability cadence to achieve fast, great results rather than lower, slower outcomes. These are not old-school back office goals – these are dynamic, tangible and genuinely inspiring to people every day. They tap into our free-will interest in reaching for great outcomes and their shorter cadence produces both more results and more satisfaction. The magic is five steps away:

Use Goals to Define and Drive Success

Goals work when they're inspiring and capture our natural intention for greatness. They should describe what great victory is for every team, and be a real-time rather than one-time rally point for people. When they're tangible, they provide purpose which improves everyone's contribution and provides a focal point for day-to-day execution. By defining clear short term goals and metrics, you've defined priorities and given people permission to focus on the most valuable activities. (Leaders often overestimate how well people understand their goals – just 7% of people really do!)

Dump the Old-School Goal Model for One that Amplifies Results

Techniques like Objectives and Key Results (OKRs) help companies achieve the best *possible* rather than the most *probable* results. This method combines bold, aspirational statements with metrics for Key Results that reflect awesome outcomes. OKRs provide *radical clarity* for everyone in the organization on what they're trying to achieve and where to spend their time – they are the tie breaker. Where traditional approaches encourage people to set the results ceiling low, OKRs amplify results by removing the ceiling and focusing on the best possible outcome. When you're maximizing the possibilities with OKRs, disconnect OKRs from performance reviews.

Manage Achievement in Real-Time

Goals and OKRs are only as good as their execution and with short range goals (as with sales), every week in a 12-week quarter matters. As business velocity accelerates, leaders can't wait for monthly and quarterly reviews to find out the team got distracted, can't overcome roadblocks or lost its way. With real-time goals and continuous execution transparency, you can help people stay goal-focused, easily predict results and drive accountability.

Make Goals as Present as Email

Your team should be able to find their goals and yours and see progress against them in 3 seconds. That's about how long it takes to focus on the last message in their inbox – which is your goal's competition for their time and focus. Our research shows that high performers start their day by looking at their goals and then consciously aligning their time with their aspirations. If you want to be a goal-focused organization, make it easy for *everyone* to focus on them every day.

Goals Should Flow Top Down and Bottom Up

Pure hierarchies rarely work today; organizations that focus on teaming and leading across each level are more agile and successful. When goals only flow top down in large organizations, opportunities—maybe even markets—are lost. Talented people and great ideas are everywhere in an organization; let their aspirations flow and you'll be unstoppable. Rather than an over-rigid down line cascade that assumes the chief knows all, converge on goals so innovation isn't stifled *and* broader strategies progress smoothly.

So How Do You Assess Performance and Decide Who Gets Pay and Promotions?

Instead of a one-time performance review event, use continuous conversations to coach and calibrate. Have 1-on-1's at least twice a month and calibrate on three things: engagement, performance and alignment. We use five levels for each and recommend both manager and employee share their view so perception gaps can be addressed quickly. End of year, your employees had 24 conversations with opportunities to improve and recognition—it's more authentic, builds skill and improves performance. Reviews are simple because the facts are shared, there are no surprises and it is just another in a series of performance conversations.

QUICK TIPS ON OKRS USE

- Set only one OKR for the company, unless you have multiple business lines. It's about focus.
- Give yourself three months for an OKR. How bold is it if you can do it in a week?
- Keep the metrics out of the Objective. The Objective is inspirational.
- In the weekly check in, open with company OKR, then do groups. Don't do every individual; that's better in private 1:1s. Which you *do* have every week, right?
- OKRs cascade; set company OKRs, then group's/roles. Don't set individual OKR.
- OKRs are not the only thing you do; they are the one thing you *must* do. Trust people to keep the ship running, and don't jam every task into your OKRs.
- The Monday OKR check in is a *conversation*. Be sure to discuss change in confidence, health metrics and priorities.
- Encourage employees to suggest company OKRs. OKRs are great bottom up, not just top down.
- Make OKRs available publicly. Google has them on their intranet.
- Friday celebrations is an antidote to Monday's grim business. Keep it upbeat!

A LITTLE HISTORY AND CREDIT WHERE CREDIT IS DUE

I first was exposed to OKRs at Zynga. The general framework of what would eventually become Objectives and Key Results came from Andy Grove implementing Peter Drucker's Management by Objective system at Intel. Then John Doerr, former Intel executive and now partner at Kleiner, Perkins, Caufield and Byers, began evangelizing them to all the startups he invested in. Some, like Google and then Zynga, embraced them fully and used them to unify and energize their companies. Those successes joined by companies like LinkedIn (who adopted OKRs after I had moved on) and General Assembly (where I taught in 2013) made OKRs an effective accelerant to their growth.

When I left Zynga, I began advising startups. I didn't see why they should have to learn everything the hard way, as I had. The first thing I noticed again and again was a painful and potentially deadly lack of focus. Even startups who had found product/market fit found it excruciating to get their employees to all work toward their vision, and with the next funding cycle always coming much too soon, they had to find a way to get everyone executing. It wasn't surprising that I turned to OKRs to help.

When I brought the Zynga-style approach to young startups, I saw they had a low tolerance for any meetings, much less a two-hour one doing deep analysis. I trimmed the meetings down to a weekly discussion around the company OKR status, followed by each team's, and that worked well. Some companies would follow it up with a metrics analysis, some with a pipeline discussion, but starting with revisiting our goals makes all the difference in making them.

Every company I've worked for has had some kind of weekly celebration, some tied with launch, others just because it's Friday. Then one day, I worked with a startup that didn't. They were just young, and it hadn't yet occurred to them that it was an important bonding ritual. So when I was able to nudge them into trying it out, I got to suggest what form it took. I had heard designers complain about being left out of the Agile ritual of Friday demos, so I thought I'd suggest everyone demo. This was amazingly transformative. Suddenly each team knew what the other team was doing and they gained respect for the other. As well, OKRs by their very nature force you to push hard and fail. The Friday celebration of success was an antidote to the hard and fierce march across a field of failed experiments all startups experience.

In the course of my research, I've spent time talking to Rick Klau, the OKR proponent from Google Ventures. The Google implementation of OKRs is quite different than the one I recommend here, and it's worth exploring the video and materials he shares. In my personal experience, the approach I lay out here is effective with most startups and mid-sized companies. But every team is different, and you should feel free to iterate.

I want to especially thank Cathy Yardley, who helped me write like a fiction author. As well, these fine folks were beta readers, and gave me a TON of advice and insight on how to make this book better:

James Cham, David Shen, Laura Klein, Richard Dalton, Abby Covert, Dan Klyn, Scott Baldwin, Angus Edwardson, Irene Au, Scott Berkun, Jorge Arango, Francis Rowland, Sandra.Kogan, A.J. Kandy, Jeff Atwood, Adam Connor, Charles Brewer, Samantha Soma, Austin Govella, Allison Cooper, Ed Lewis, Brad Dickason, Pamela Drouin, David Holl, Stacy-Marie Ishmael, Kim Forthofer, Derek Featherston, Jason Alderman, Ammneh Azeim, Adam Polansky, Joe Sohkol, Brandy Porter, Bethany Stole, Susan Mercer, Kevin Hoffman, Francis Storr, Leonard Burton, Elizabeth Buie, Dave Malouf, Josh Porter, Klaus Kaasgaard, Evan Litvak, Katy Law, Erin Malone, Justin Ponczek, Erin Hoffman, Elizabeth Ibarra, Harry Max, Tanya Siadneva, Casey Kawahara, Jack Kolokus, Maria Leticia Saramentos-Santos, Hannah Kim, Brittany Metz, Laura Deel, Kelly Fadem, Francis Nakagawa, An Nguyen, and you, the person I forgot to list, you were the most helpful of all and you can yell at me next time we see each other.

Read on for an excerpt from Christina Wodtke's new fable,

The Team That Managed Itself

"Baby needs a new pair of shoes!" Allie screamed.

Rob laughed out loud at that. "Really?"

She threw the dice. "When in Vegas, roll like you're in Vegas! You got to live every damn movie cliché!"

Rob nodded. Her best friend might be sober and keeping his money off the table, but he was whooping and cheering with their team. Tonight, they were celebrating.

"Snake eyes!" the croupier announced.

The table groaned, and the dice passed to George.

"Let me show you how it's done, honey," purred the studio general manager.

Allie had a sudden sense of perfection, like a key snapping into a lock. She had her best friend on one side, and her dream boss on the other. Rob was a tall African American, and Allie was a tiny mestizo. George was something and Chinese, and even if they didn't look like the usual bro-co team, they had managed to snare the third quarter of top earnings at SOS. And they had done it all with a game that was basically Minecraft with quilting squares—a girly game. Allie wished the first-person shooter fanboys she went to high school with could see her now.

Allie placed her bet next to Rob and George's. Why not? Her bet on QuiltWorld was winning, as it had been for months now.

Then her phone vibrated against her hip, where she had stuck it in the waistband of her skirt. She didn't dare leave it in her purse in the noisy casino. Weekend or not, she was always on call.

She pulled it out and looked. Midnight stats were in.

"Easy fours!" called the croupier.

Yep, George had gotten her another win. Allie grabbed her chips and stepped back from the table to look at her game's numbers.

As lead product manager on top-earning mobile game QuiltWorld, it was her right to be here in Vegas with the team. They had blown away revenue expectations and her CEO Rick had rewarded the QuiltWorld team with a trip to Vegas. But as lead PM, she still needed to keep an eye on numbers, in case something went sideways. Her boss could chill out and get drunk, because he knew his team had his back.

Plus, she wanted to watch the numbers. She was excited. She had crafted a new bold beat—a special event designed for the game—under the tutelage of the lead game designer. She was dying to see how it performed. She didn't consider herself creative, not like the game designers or the art team, but she had correlated numbers across the various games in the studio and had seen a pattern that inspired a fresh idea.

In late summer, all the games at SOS got the doldrums. Their biggest competitor was a sunny day. Games that spoke to the desire to play in the sun could get a lift midafternoon in the workday. You can't sneak outside, but you can sneak a peek at a pretend outdoors on your computer. Allie had come up with an idea that was all about playing outside on a playground, with swings and slides and a baseball field. They packaged it up as a "sewing kit"— QuiltWorld's name for mini-expansions to the game— and offered it to players so they could make their own playground.

QuiltWorld was a strange beast inside of SOS. SOS had started out as just another game company trying to ride the popularity wave of mobile games. They began with a combination of gambling and pulp-fiction inspired games. Vampires, cops and robbers, gangsters. But then a tiny mythical group— George, Pete, and Christie—had a new idea. They took the popularity of a sandbox game, where you take modular units and build things with them, and rethemed it with quilts. It was Minecraft, but with quilts. The CEO Rick had thought it was the stupidest idea he'd ever seen, but because it was George, and George had a track record at another company of taking stupid ideas and making a lot of money from them, he'd funded it—given them their time, plus an engineer and a game artist to make the images. They launched an alpha and the numbers were beyond any anyone had seen. Players went insane for it. Rick still couldn't understand it, but it didn't stop him from taking credit for it.

QuiltWorld was now the biggest studio in SOS, dwarfing even Baccarat. SOS had cloned the core concept to great success. ClayTown, another sandbox game but themed on claymation, was the second biggest, and Sketchworld was the up-and-comer. Rick was overjoyed. A serial entrepreneur, he always told them at company meetings that SOS was what his entire life had led up to, and they would be reinventing the very nature of fun. He was so proud he was able to be profitable and respectable at the same time.

The Vegas trip tradition came from the time when all the games at SOS were on the sleazy end of respectability. You made the most money, you got to go to Vegas. No matter how many times at the company meetings Rick talked about "forever games" and "innovation" and "high quality production," what got you to Vegas was revenue. At SOS, a good game was a game that made money.

George lost the dice and peeled back from the table. "Waitress hasn't been by in a while. Want to get a drink?"

The two of them wove through the crowded casino. When they had claimed the craps table, the casino was sparsely populated by a handful of dedicated gamblers. Now every square inch of floor space had a human on it. The bar itself was also lined with humanity—drinking, laughing, flirting. An unrepentantly cheesy piano man swore to play any song for the right tip.

Allie wedged her way in near a tall middle-aged man and leaned in to get the bartender's attention. In her outstretched hand she held a twenty, in case money was a better bartender lure than cleavage. The man next to her caught notice.

"Hey, where you from?" Vegas's standard opening line, from hawkers on the sidewalks to men at bars.

Allie was used to a bit too much attention. Her hard to place ethnic features and hip-length black hair were a magnet for certain kinds of men.

"She's with me," George said, placing an arm on her shoulder. The man turned away with the complacency of the unsober.

"Ew!" Allie laughed, shrugging George's arm off her. "What will your wife say?"

"She'll say I'm watching out for you."

The bartender finally swung by and got their order. Allie ordered two shots of Patron.

"So, we're toasting?" asked George.

"Toasting what?" grinned back Allie. She gestured at the Patron.

"You got the midnight numbers. I can look at them on my phone, or you can tell me."

"SummerQuest is doing quite well. Even in the evening, we're up 8 percent!"

George offered a hand for a high five, and

Allie smacked it. They turned to their shots and downed them.

"Good work, half-pint! You've got a knack for this!"

"Ah, the numbers just like me. They tell me their secrets."

"The number whisperer." George ordered a margarita. "Never mix, never worry."

Allie ordered a soda water. She believed drinking was like a game: It was all about pacing. She looked back at the table where her team played on. They screamed as one and went into an impromptu wave.

"We're going to get kicked out," she said.

"No way," George replied. "It's Vegas, baby. To QuiltWorld!"

They clicked glasses merrily.

Allie felt a tap on her shoulder. Where her admirer had stood now was a middle-aged woman. She was perhaps from the south, with very tall hair and a thick layer of makeup. "Excuse me, but did I hear you work on QuiltWorld?"

"Why, yes," Allie replied. George's smile faded from his eyes, though it remained on his lips.

"Oh, I love that game! My quilts are so beautiful. I work on them every day when the kids are at school!"

"Have you tried Original Martha?"

"Oh my God!" she squealed. "Oh, gracious, didn't mean to curse! I love it so much! It was like traveling back in time."

Allie heard George mutter, "Not quite."

"I felt so patriotic, like I was part of history! And so good of you to donate to history education. My sister made her first in-app purchase to help out!"

Allie shot George a look. It was her idea to use a donation element to up in-app purchases. It had bumped revenue, got positive PR, and raised money for history books for public schools.

George returned her look with one that said, "Okay, okay," with a slight eyeroll.

"Would you like to see my quilt?"

"See it?" Allie responded.

"I have my iPad! I took screenshots!"

"I'd love to," Allie said quite sincerely.

George stepped back, then off toward the table. Pete, his CTO, greeted him with a fist bump and a bro-hug. Pete's mass almost knocked George over. Allie was glad to not participate in the ritual. She preferred spending time with her players. The woman showed her screenshots of her quilt structures, including the quilted White House that was part of the Fourth of July bold beat, and then showed off her QuiltWorld towns. She had two—one a miniature

New York and one that looked like a small midwestern town. She must have spent a fortune over the years on these.

"I'm trying to make my hometown," she admitted shyly. "I know some people take apart the kits and make their own QTs," she said, pronouncing it "cuties,"" "and I thought I'd try to do it, too."

"It's darling! Is your house here?" Allie asked, fascinated. *Is this common?* She thought rolling-your-own was an advanced player trick, but if it was spreading, then maybe they should consider how to build that in for more players.

"It's right here." The woman smiled widely, yet Allie could see she was anxious about sharing her work.

"Wow, you did that!" Allie knew there was only one right response when a creator was brave enough to share.

Now the woman was beaming. "Sure did! I actually found our house's blueprints, you know, to get ideas for how to make it. You see here, I'm using some of the Valentine's Day kit to get the lattice work on the porch right!"

"That is beautiful." Allie sighed. She meant it. The house was fine, but what was beautiful was this woman finding her way to creativity and the pride of making something new. That's why she loved working on QuiltWorld. When she met the players and found they were unlocking their creativity, she felt proud. And perhaps a little jealous. But mostly proud.

Her phone vibrated. She ignored it for a second, but it vibrated again and again. A call. She smiled at the woman. "I have to take this," she said, and moved toward what she hoped was a quieter corner of the casino as she answered, "Jenova."

It was Noam, one of the engineering pod leaders. He had volunteered to stay behind to mind the shop because "I hate Vegas. It's a pit of despair."

He sounded tense. "The new bold beat is in freefall. We can't tell if it's a reporting problem or a bug in the back end. I just know everything's testing fine here. Can you grab Rob or Pete?"

Allie pivoted and headed toward the table. She tapped Rob, her lead dev, on the shoulder. He looked up as she said into the phone, "Okay, we'll poke around and get back to you."

Rob gave her a look that said, "Of course." He shook his head and walked away. He didn't gamble, but he believed deeply and completely in the importance of spending face time with his team and was sad to have to step away from the celebration. They walked to the elevators.

"I can't really tell much from my phone," Allie said. "But Noam is right, something isn't working. There is no way our numbers can be taking such a severe hit. I really hope it's a reporting error or I'll be having fun explaining this to Rick Monday."

Rob punched the number 32 on the console,

and the elevator smoothly ascended. Allie's ears popped.

He sighed deeply. "Something always breaks. If George would give us time to work on code rot, instead of always chasing the next bold beat, we could elevate and maintain all of our numbers instead of this moronic roller coaster ride."

"You've made that argument."

"So I have."

George's counterargument was that a dead game with good code was not as valuable as a spaghetti code that made money.

They walked to Rob's room, and he sat at his laptop on the small desk. Allie eyed the two beds, one made neatly, and one covered with jeans and T-shirts celebrating game releases.

"You're sharing with Pete?"

"Why not? He doesn't sleep at night while he's in Vegas. It's a lot like no roommate at all. Plus, I think it comforts Marie to know I'm rooming with comic book guy."

"Fair. Can I help?"

"Not yet. Hold on."

Rob played his laptop like a jazz pianist. Allie sat on the edge of the clean bed and flipped through her emails on her phone. There were no clues. Her eyes wandered over to the T-shirts. Pete had been at

SOS since the beginning and wore nothing but SOS release T-shirts as a badge of honor. She saw one on the bed from six years ago, before she'd joined, once a dark blue but now a faded sky blue. His first big hit. He must've worn it a lot to remind people what he'd accomplished. SOS had no memory, so it was probably a decent strategy. The blue shirt was the size of a small blanket, probably a triple X—as Pete liked to joke he was. He was a walking caricature of an old-school nerd. She sighed and thumbed back through the midnight numbers. Might as well bask in the one thing that was going right.

"Got it. API change. Give me a second . . ." He typed, then snapped his lid shut. His lips pressed together hard, like he was struggling to hold back a string of obscenities.

"I can announce the fix then?" she asked.

"Yes. But it will break again. This," he waved his hands in frustration over his laptop, as if it held the entire code base of QuiltWorld, "is a frigging house of cards. One strong breeze . . ." His voice trailed off as he contemplated the various ways it could break next.

Allie was taken aback. Rob never swore. Never showed anger. She knew he was unhappy about the state of QuiltWorld's code and ached to fix it. There was nothing quite so alarming as when a quiet man was angry. She ducked back to her phone to forward his fix and add a few notes.

When she looked up, his anger had passed

like a tropical storm.

"Sorry," he said. "I just don't think this is how one should run a technical team."

"No need to apologize," she replied. "Shall we head back?" She noticed Rob was absent-mindedly rubbing his left forearm, his fingers kneading into the muscles afflicted with carpal tunnel. She didn't know if he was in pain just now, or this was an anxiety reflex. She knew that even if his face was calm, his mind wasn't.

"Go ahead. I'd like to take a moment to look over the fix again." He looked at her blandly, but she wasn't fooled.

"Sure. Later!"

As Allie rode down the elevator, she wondered if they really deserved to be celebrating tonight. Her ears popped.

Sunday Afternoon

Allie got out of the shuttle van and waved at her teammates as they dispersed, some heading to the parking garage, some calling for rides. None of them had slept much; more than a few were still drunk. It had been an amazing weekend. She had spent the entire night at the craps table and left seventy-five bucks up. She didn't care about the win, but she loved craps. There was camaraderie in screaming at dice together.

She looked up at the SOS building and sighed. It'd feel good to go home, but she really wanted to run a couple of database queries before Derek picked her up after his softball game. She looked at her watch. 3:20. Yeah, she could sneak in an hour of work.

She paused indecisively for a moment and looked again at the concrete building. It was shaped a bit like an early game controller, two rounded towers connected by a lower flat building. It was mostly glass, a giant '80s style post-modernist monument. It had held Sega at one point, and then had been broken into smaller offices when they moved to cheaper property. Shiny Object Syndrome, or SOS as it was known to all, had started in a single office on the third floor, now owned the first through the third floor on the left hand of the controller, and was negotiating to own the entire building. She started to trudge toward the front door when she recognized the man standing outside of it.

"Derek!"

Her husband walked toward her, swift yet unhurried, and swept her up in his arms. "Darling, you smell like an ashtray!"

"Flatterer! You could have waited until I got home and showered." He looked fresh as a daisy. "Shouldn't you be at your game?"

"I didn't dare let you go upstairs. I knew if I didn't collect you, I'd be eating another pizza alone."

"Not after a weekend away!"

"Maybe." He put an arm around her. "Anyhow, here I am."

"Here you are." Her arm fit nicely around his waist, and she squeezed him. He was a solidly built blond, a blend of the British Isles and something that let him tan rather than burn in the sun. He didn't approve of the team trips to Vegas, either personally or professionally. SOS frowned on bringing spouses—said it interfered with team bonding, though Allie suspected it was cheapness. And while he trusted her to stay out of trouble, he found it questionable that they'd go on a business trip to a place committed to a variety of sins. He'd put on his HR hat to complain that it was unfair to addicts or put on his husband hat to complain it was yet more time he didn't get to spend with her.

"You know, I'd like to go lie by the pool with

a daiquiri and catch a show." His husband hat was jealous in a variety of ways.

Allie decided to defuse the issue. "Why don't we just go sometime? It's a short flight."

"My birthday is next month." He looked down at her and fluttered his eyelashes.

"Be a good boy until then and we'll see."

"Hmmp."

Thirty minutes into the drive, they'd finished catching up and he started fiddling around with his phone to get music playing.

"Stop that, it's dangerous."

"Not as dangerous as your taste."

"No, dearest, it isn't. Drive." She grabbed the device away from him and put on one of his playlists.

After a few moments, he spoke up again. "I really don't like it, you know."

Allie turned the music down. "I know. You know it's good for team morale."

"Abusive spouses always separate their victims from friends and family."

"It's one weekend a month when we are the top-earning team! Hardly a plot."

"Maybe. But when you have your own company, you won't take them to Vegas, will you?"

"No. I'll take them to Disneyland."

"And you'll take me?"

"Every time." She gave his knee a light squeeze. *When* she had her own company. *If* was more like it. She grew up in East Palo Alto, on the wrong side of this very highway they were driving on. On her left, her family. On the right, Stanford and all the startups it fathered. Instead of attending Stanford, she had taken over her half-brother's Nintendo when he'd grown bored with it, and his computer when he moved to New York, and then used the Internet to teach herself what she needed to get a customer service job at Hurricane, the best game company in the country (in her opinion).

Then she just worked harder than everyone else and look at her now. No degree, but hey, enough stock options to be a millionaire if the IPO went well. She just needed to keep hustling and eventually, she'd get promoted to general manager. Then she'd know enough to finally found her own start-up. She was living the Silicon Valley dream.

Rob Leaving QuiltWorld

At 7 a.m., SOS felt deserted to Allie. The parking lot held a half-dozen cars, so she knew someone was here, which made the office even more eerie. The front door was locked, so she swiped in with her keycard. There was no receptionist at the front desk. The grand staircase could hold more than a hundred people at a time and did when they took their annual year-end photo. She hopped up the stairs, eschewing the elevator, eking out what exercise she could from the office since who knew when she'd get to the gym. Her mind chattered at her, avoiding the question of how to explain the latest numbers dip to her CEO. The kindest thing one could say about Rick was that he was mercurial. She'd seen him go from delighted to incensed in seconds. He was determined, ambitious, and driven by inner demons without names, and had built up SOS from zero to six hundred people in under three years.

He had an unerring instinct for trends and drove everyone faster and faster trying to stay on top of each opportunity as it appeared, generally succeeding. She had learned more in her two years there than her entire career before and had paid in blood. It was clear that the payments were not stopping anytime soon.

Allie walked into the studio. A glance around the open space showed only one person in the cavernous room. SOS eschewed cubes in favor of tables in rows with computers on each table. It had a sweatshop for nerds quality. Rob called it the panopticon—a prison where you were always watched. And Rob was the room's sole occupant. Most of the engineering crew stayed until 2 a.m. most nights and wandered in around ten. Rob preferred silence to program, so he'd become a lark rather than a night owl. On a launch night, she'd still be there when he came in at 5 a.m. She'd learned that just because he came in that early didn't mean he wanted to talk to people at that hour. She looked at him as she entered, and he gave her a slight nod, suggesting perhaps he'd had enough coffee to be social. That made one of them.

She dropped her coat at her desk and headed to the break room to pour a second cup. She heard Rob come up behind her.

"What's brought you in before ten? I thought you resolved the dB error?" Rob's face showed only the slightest trace of concern.

"Metrics meeting."

Rob winced. "I thought that was on Thursday."

"Rick moved it."

"Again? Typical." Rob looked into his milky coffee. "Heya, so, I wanted to ask you something."

ABOUT THE AUTHOR

Christina Wodtke trains companies to move from insight to execution as principal of her firm, Wodtke Consulting, and teaches the next generation of entrepreneurs at Stanford.

Christina has led redesigns and initial product offerings for such companies as LinkedIn, Myspace, Zynga, Yahoo!, Hot Studio, and eGreetings. She has founded two consulting startups, a product startup, and Boxes and Arrows, an online magazine of design; and she co-founded the Information Architecture Institute.

She speaks everywhere from conferences to universities to boardrooms, and opines across the internet, but most often on eleganthack.com.

Made in the USA
Coppell, TX
29 September 2020

38926760R00104